TOO MUCH
TUSCAN SUN

TOO MUCH
TUSCAN SUN

Confessions of a Chianti Tour Guide

Dario Castagno
with Robert Rodi

GUILFORD, CONNECTICUT

To Raymond Flower

(A REAL GENTLEMAN)

■■
■■

Text design: Lisa Reneson, www.twosistersdesign.com
Cover design: Diana Nuhn
Cover photo: © Masterfile
Author photograph: © Dorian Trifiro
Rooster art on inside front and back covers: © Stockart.com

Library of Congress Cataloging-in-Publication Data is available.

ISBN 0-7627-3670-4

Manufactured in the United States of America
First Edition/Second Printing

CONTENTS

CONTENTS

But if you come I shall pour for you
Etruscan Chianti similar to ruby,
that kisses you and bites you
and makes you shed sweet tears

Fulvio Testi (1593–1646)

RINGRAZIAMENTI

What a bore. There was exactly nothing on television, and Cristina and I were twiddling our thumbs on the sofa, staring blankly at the ceiling, its white expanse interrupted here and there by spiderwebs. The dog was stretched out on his mat, mirroring our mood: dull, inert, apathetic.

"Why don't we begin work on the book?" I asked. "Why not?" Cristina replied with a shrug. For a while we'd discussed the idea of writing a book about my experiences as a tour guide, though till now we hadn't taken the project very seriously. But from this night on, for almost two years, we spent every evening applying ourselves to the task. At first it was almost in the nature of a pastime, but slowly, as the book began to take shape, our commitment deepened. Each night I dug through my memory, searching for incidents and situations that would in some way cohere with and amplify the rest of the work.

Accordingly, I must thank first of all Cristina, who, in the midst of working her regular job and studying for her degree, had the patience to sit night after night before the computer, waiting for my recollections to come. At the beginning there were long stretches when they didn't come at all. With the passage of time, though, events flowed more easily back to my memory, and

I was revisited by remembrances of clients and excursions that had almost faded with time. These rediscoveries were very enjoyable—yet at the same time a bit poignant, because they made me aware of exactly how much time had passed since my first tour.

Cristina's involvement has been fundamental. Without her collaboration I would never have been able to write these pages. It would have been entirely correct to include her name on the cover; but editorial conventions will have their way.

Thanks also to my friend Chuck, who suggested the title.

My thanks go as well to my ever-colorful clients, who are the true protagonists of this work. I consider myself particularly fortunate to have worked above all with Americans. Had I engaged primarily with tourists of some other nationality, I would by now very likely have changed careers. The enthusiasm and kindness of my American customers gave me the will to continue, year after year, mile after mile, without ever becoming bored.

During the two years of writing, I continued each day escorting clients, always hoping to encounter someone new and interesting, or to receive bizarre requests that I could include in the book. I was not disappointed. All the names of my customers, however, have been changed to protect their privacy—with the exception of a special few who have given explicit permission. I must also thank Raymond Flower, an English gentleman, one of the first to have come to live among the hills of Chianti, who has loved this countryside fervently and who, without knowing it, helped me build this enterprise from nothing.

Thanks as well to the Noble *Contrada* of the Caterpillar, who welcomed me into their number with open arms, making me feel at last a true (and proud) Sienese.

After producing a first draft in Italian, I translated this book into English during a vacation in Spain. Notwithstanding my long familiarity with the language of Albion, the result was not of the highest degree; it required the touch of a professional. My thanks, then, to three bottles of Chianti Classico, drained during a succulent dinner on a mild Sienese night. It was thanks to this nectar of Bacchus that, while slightly inebriated, I asked Robert Rodi if he was interested in taking on the project. Frankly, I hadn't expected that a writer from across the ocean would be as enthusiastic as Robert was; in fact, the following morning, I thought suddenly that the agreement so readily reached the night before might as quickly have been forgotten, as often occurs after a bit of Chianti. But as the sages say, *in vino veritas,* and on this occasion the adage could not be more appropriate.

From that day a working correspondence began between Robert and me, which has resulted in this definitive English version of the book.

FOREWORD

Americans through Tuscan Eyes

In the past few years, as more and more books about Tuscany have been published, it has become almost impossible to enter a bookshop without being confronted by a sprawling array of volumes dedicated to the area. As always, there are the standard guidebooks choked with hotel and restaurant recommendations, cookbooks devoted to the specialties of the Tuscan table, and lavish photo books in which the rolling Tuscan landscape is immortalized.

But the genre seems recently to have been reenergized by an innovation among its ranks. I'm talking about books written by intrepid foreigners, those who have spent time here—or in some cases picked up and relocated here—then decided to write about their experiences. Often these are amusing and diverting memoirs in which the author discusses his or her discovery of Tuscany's bounty, perplexity at the difference in local customs, purchase and painstaking rehabilitation of an old property, the still-audible echoes of historical events, or quite simply the paradisiacal remoteness of the countryside from the frenetic imperatives of city life.

I enjoy reading these accounts, especially when they describe in such starry-eyed detail the rhythms of our lives, our habits and customs, and the quaintness of our local "characters." Having lived here for much of my life, it still amuses me that the matter-of-fact patterns of our daily existence can seem so dazzlingly exotic when viewed through the eyes of a foreigner. As recently as twenty years ago, if you'd told a Tuscan peasant whose dream was to go to America that his dilapidated old farmhouse would soon become the dream home of wealthy Americans, the peasant would have considered you just this side of a lunatic.

But this revolution has indeed occurred. Indeed, I sometimes get the impression that it is sufficient to insert the word *Tuscany* into the title of any book to obtain its passport to the American best-seller lists. With this in mind, and without intending any slight to those writers who have come before me, I humbly propose that it's time for a genuine Tuscan to enter the fray.

Accordingly, I've written a book offering just the opposite point of view: that of a native Tuscan, reporting on the wave of enthusiastic Americans surging ever more strongly onto his beachhead. I am perhaps in a better position than most to take on this task: As a professional tour guide for more than a dozen years, I have made my living by escorting small groups of tourists through the Chianti region, which lies at the heart—both geographically and culturally—of Tuscany.

If you haven't read a book on Tuscany before, this one will still serve as an introduction. In its pages I will offer you a portrait of my home as I've come to know it—with my own views on its history, culture, and character. I'll also take you through a typical year as experienced by a native. And laced throughout the narrative will be an account of my more remarkable experiences with my most memorable American customers.

This is not intended as any kind of vendetta against those American authors who have, despite their love for our people, exhibited some relish in detailing our peculiarities, tics, manias, pathologies, and various seasonal madnesses. But if I achieve something similarly risible in my portrayal of my American clients, please keep in mind the spirit of mutual discovery and affection with which I write.

This seems a suitable point at which to thank all those who have recommended my services to their friends, thus providing me the means to continue making my living in daily contact with the earth I love the most—and, in turn, providing me with the material for this endeavor. My gratitude, on both counts, is heartfelt.

TOO MUCH TUSCAN SUN

DISCOVERING CHIANTI

I confess at the outset I'm not a native-born *chiantigiano*: I was born in England. My parents, both Italians, met in London, where they had moved for career reasons. There they were married and produced first my brother, then me, before returning to Italy to put down roots in Chianti for good. I was ten at the time—just old enough to have learned English fluently before starting my new life in Tuscany. Now, after twenty-five years in this splendid territory, I think I can call myself *chiantigiano* without fear of rebuttal. I have none of the expatriate's conflicting affections; London, while fondly remembered, feels increasingly remote. The place I recognize in my heart as home is this one.

When I was a newborn, my Italian relatives said I resembled Winston Churchill; the English neighbors said Benito Mussolini. In London as a child, I attended a typical English public school founded on rigid indoctrination and discipline, which succeeded in making me quite a little British toff—perfectly integrated into the ossified English social hierarchy. When my parents advised me that we would be leaving England for Italy, I was deeply upset and made innumerable attempts to get them to change their minds. I believed, as most British do (or did), that everything outside that sceptered isle was primitive and underdeveloped. Once in Italy, I was convinced, I would pine for all the wonderful things I was leaving behind: ginger biscuits dipped in tea, hours passed on the cricket fields waiting for a chance to touch the ball, the aroma of burned marshmallows roasted on the kitchen fire—even my itchy, ill-fitting school uniform suddenly seemed an absolutely crucial part of my identity.

But of course I was young, and so fascinated was I by the new world I was given to explore that I quickly forgot my London ways. Actually, the most significant culture shock wasn't the change from one country to another, but moving from a city of twelve million to a village of two thousand. I had never lived in the country before, and while at the callow age of ten I wasn't yet able to appreciate the glories of the landscape that surrounded me, I certainly appreciated the chance to spend hours each day beneath an open sky, completely at liberty.

The Tuscan countryside in the 1970s was the perfect playground for a child: enormous spaces in which to roam and not much in the way of danger (road traffic being nearly nonexistent). And the school schedule left us our afternoons free. What a dizzying change from my tightly regulated English school days! My classmates put me immediately at ease and, with the adaptability of youth, I soon became a typical *toscanaccio*.

In fact, I may have felt this liberation too keenly. At fifteen I was expelled from school for poor marks and undisciplined behavior. Soon I found myself working at a large winery in the area. There was of course no public transportation to take me to and from my job, so my parents bought me a small light blue Vespa, and it was with this vehicle that I first started exploring the countryside. Freed from the limitations of my skeletal old bicycle, I began leaving the main thoroughfares, spending all my spare time following the many unpaved, winding white roads that crisscross Chianti like stitching. And each time, I was impressed by the number of abandoned farmhouses I encountered. Some were easily accessible and in fairly good shape, others on the brink of collapse, still others virtually unreachable and covered by vegetation. Ignoring the fact that it was forbidden to enter, I began to investigate those old houses; I found them to be quite lovely. This game soon became a passion that I have never lost.

In those days such old houses were considered of no real value. Often my friends mocked my habit of spending entire solitary weekends traveling from ruin to worthless ruin. "Why waste your time searching out old dumps?" they'd ask. "Can't you see they're all the same?" In a sense this was true. Certainly at first sight the similarities were striking: All were built from stone, with terra-cotta tile roofs and ceilings supported by chestnut beams. All had exterior chicken coops, ground-level stables, and bedrooms on the second floor, with a well in the courtyard and a barn on the opposite side. But to a practiced eye, each was in some way unique, with a different physiognomy, like a fingerprint left behind by the peasant who had constructed and lived in it. Every time I entered one, even if I found only shrouds of cobweb and bats hidden in the fireplace, I could sense the history of the people who were born, lived, and died within its walls—their spirits often seemed still to linger there. I was so taken by these old homesteads that often I would go to the nearest bar and strike up conversations with old men who might remember something about the house and family. Sometimes I succeeded in finding the former inhabitants themselves; they were invariably amused by my interest. And some of them, sipping a glass of grappa and puffing on a Tuscan cigar, relished telling me the thousand-and-one stories that those houses hid. I would listen for hours, mesmerized.

The majority of the inhabitants abandoned the houses during the postwar period of massive industrialization and moved to the nearby towns, where a network of small industries was developing. As the farms emptied, town centers burgeoned. As fast as mushrooms after a rainfall, apartment buildings sprang up, boasting all the modern comforts. Running water, central heating, and indoor bathrooms were luxuries that peasants had only dreamed about—now, suddenly, they could afford to possess them. It's easy today, seeing those splendid stone houses transformed into lavish and comfortable holiday homes, to criticize the choices of those peasants, but theirs was a grindingly tough life of labor from sunup to sundown, leaving little room for any sort of romance.

The paradox, of course, is that I found in the ashes of their lives a romance that was well-nigh irresistible.

JANUARY AND THE ATHLETES

A month of cold, clear days occasionally warmed by a soft sun, ferocious eastern winds, light rains, and windy storms. The landscape is largely muted: gray, brown, purplish, smoky blue. Chianti is limestone country where patches of vine weave between thick forests, bushes, and rocky hills only partly covered by scrub, brooms, and ferns.

The hills are divided by five deep valleys in which the main rivers flow: Pesa, Greve, Arbia, Ombrone, and Staggia. Here the vegetation is luxurious, rich in poplars and willows. In the smaller valleys the rivers are dry for most of the year, but they become impetuous torrents soon after the rainstorms.

The forests are mainly oak, mixed with chestnut, pine, and beech. The oak loses its leaves, but there is a gray cast to the forest given by the foliage of the evergreens—trees like juniper, pine, and ilex. Color also erupts from the tips of the Spanish broom, the crimson stems of the omnipresent dogwood, and orange clumps of willow. Splendid lichens splash the landscape with yellow, orange, and olive green.

In the garden the first snowdrops and winter jasmines bloom. On colder days the squirrels chatter and quarrel while jumping tree to tree, greedily consuming pinecones. Their coats, initially reddish in this season, become darker, nearly black. At night the porcupine often emerges in search of food. The dog hears him, but pretends not to. He's been pierced by those vicious quills before, and prefers now to stay away.

On the bare branches sit tiny, trembling birds—sparrows, thrushes, blackbirds, and robins—alert, timid, and very cautious. Who can fault their reticence? So many fall prey to the area's numerous predators.

The month of January is, for me, a slow one; the great mass of tourists waits for spring before flooding into Tuscany. Country hotels, inns, and tour offices take advantage of this dead period to clean up and do little, long-delayed chores to prepare for the new season. Only the large urban hotels, though far from booked to capacity, always seem to have some occupied rooms. Visiting the art-laden cities in this period can be a good choice: The prices are lower, the restaurants don't require reservations, and museum entrances don't confront you with the stressful, miles-long lines typical of the high season. The staff at the tourist information bureaus are more likely to be helpful, and the waiters at the restaurants are both able and happy to dedicate more time to you, without the burden of many additional tables full of hungry and demanding tourists.

True, the days are often very cold, but with a little bit of luck you'll find yourself enjoying a suitably mild spell. Winters here are usually dry, heavy showers being much less likely than in spring or fall. Only the area's famous gardens are best avoided completely; in this period, they're moribund and sleepy.

It appeals to me to walk in Siena in January. The city once again becomes the property of the Sienese, and it's possible to take a stroll along the main street without crashing into one of those huge groups of tourists all wearing the same hat. In high season such groups move about the city en masse, like a great flock of sheep following not a shepherd's crook but a brightly colored umbrella.

Siena is a fascinating city to which, in my opinion, visitors often give short shrift. Most people seem more intent on admiring the art and architecture of its more famous neighbor, Florence. For this reason, many visitors limit their time in Siena to a few hours, just enough to see a few of the major attractions: the Piazza del Campo, the Duomo, the main street, possibly a museum. Few people are aware that in the thirteenth century, Siena was a prominent center of Europe, and that currently it is one of the largest and best-preserved medieval cities in Italy.

Only by adventuring into its hundreds of alleys, wandering without any particular destination or hurry, can you discover the near infinity of public squares and churches, evocative and mysterious corners unknown to the average tourist. This is what I like to propose to my clients—a walking tour through the manifold beauties of Siena, far afield from the confusion and hubbub of the established tourist sites, but closer to the true spirit of the city.

It was in January that I received, from a couple named Franklin, a request to take them on just such a tour. We worked out all the details via fax, and on a certain Sunday morning I went to pick them up at a quaint little hotel outside the city's ancient walls. Fortunately the day was splendid: the sky an intense blue, completely clear of clouds, the climate frigid but dry, and the sun just strong enough to provide a pleasant, cozy warmth in areas away from the wind. The bells of the hundreds of churches were ringing wildly, and the echo in the little private parking lot was deafening. The bells seemed almost frantic to persuade the faithful to go and render homage to the Lord; empty churches are sadly typical of Italy at the turn of the millennium.

I met the Franklins while they were leaving the hotel's breakfast room. I was able to pinpoint them immediately, since there appeared to be no other guests in the hotel. "You must be Dario," they said in tandem. "Excuse us while we grab some things from the room; we'll join you back here in just a sec." During the short wait I sat down and skimmed through the local daily paper, in which the main story, printed in giant cubic letters on the front page, informed citizens of the damages caused by pigeon excrement. I had only read half this piece, neither amused nor particularly interested in the stomach acids of birds, when the Franklins returned to the lobby each holding a PowerBar in the left hand and a Diet Coke in the right.

"We want to see the whole city, like you promised in your fax. We're athletes, we jog every day and do aerobics, so we aren't afraid if we have to walk a little." They had a pleasant, friendly look about them—in fact, as often happens to couples who live together a long time, they looked rather a lot alike. I guessed both to be about fifty. Each was tall and robust, and from beneath their New York Yankees caps some white hair spilled over their ears. They had florid red faces and wide shoulders, and their muscular legs were widely out of proportion to the rest of their bodies, with NBA-sized feet lashed into equally gigantic Nike sports shoes. They wore identical jogging suits of the same model and manufacturer, both in improbable colors: baby-girl pink for her, baby-boy blue for him. The sweetest and most improbable thing about them was the childlike smiles splayed across their faces—smiles that caused ripples above their eyebrows and creases in their cheeks. Their facial muscles must have endured more than a little stress in their continuous effort to sustain this expression of surprised delight.

I began the tour, as usual, by relating some of the city's ancient legends and reciting a sequence of names and dates. The Franklins seemed very enthusiastic and interested; gratifyingly, they laughed at my jokes and asked all sorts of questions.

As soon as we entered the old city walls through the imposing Porta Romana, we turned into the territory of the Mutton (each district of Siena has its own distinct mascot), where our walk would begin. When they saw the steep climb we had ahead of us, they asked if there was any way to avoid it. When I said, "I don't think so," Mrs. Franklin's perpetual smile at long last wilted. Looking into my eyes imploringly, she inquired how many other hills we would have to climb during the tour. "Well," I explained, "Siena is constructed on three hills, and therefore to visit it properly requires going up and down often. But since nobody is chasing us, we can stop for breathers anytime you like." I was a bit worried by this unexpected change in my customers' humor. To forestall any useless argument, I reminded them that during our contacts via fax they had reserved a walking tour, and that on walking tours it is almost inevitable that you will have to walk. Then, to boost their confidence, I said, "And after all, you're athletes, aren't you?"

But in truth I was a little alarmed. What worried me most was that from the departure point we had so far covered perhaps three hundred yards, and they seemed already exhausted; they were panting like dogs, heads drooping, keeping themselves upright only by propping themselves against a wall, as though they'd just completed a marathon.

While I tried to think of some solution to this embarrassing situation, providence came to my aid. A very old woman, bone-thin, shrouded in black, approached us clenching four enormous shopping bags in her frail little fists. Paying heed to neither the weight of her bags nor the incline of the ascent, she began climbing the slope with a steady, determined gait, all the while keeping tight between her lips a cigarette that she puffed efficiently, inhaling and exhaling smoke without ever stopping to take it from her mouth. She passed us with such rapidity as to make even a teenager envy her energy, greeting us with a short but eloquent nod. The Franklins stood rooted for a moment, amazed by the physical prowess of this bony old lady, who soon become nothing more than a black dot at the top of the street. Without further discussion we continued our walking tour.

The street led to the church of Santa Maria dei Servi, where we enjoyed a breathtaking view of the old city. Then we descended into the Shell district, where the Franklins opened one of their Diet Cokes and shared it. We continued through the Unicorn to the Tower, where they consumed the other, just before visiting the cramped, hidden Jewish synagogue tucked away in one of the alleys of this district.

Having reached the immortal Piazza del Campo, the nexus of all social life in Siena, we took a seat in one of the cafes situated around the square to order some refreshment. I chose a beer; they, obviously, a Diet Coke. Apart from the drinks the tour was proceeding rather well, with neither difficulties nor delays: Thanks to the example of the providential old woman, the Franklins gamboled up and down the hilly streets like mountain goats, their beautiful child-smiles stamped on their faces. We continued our explorations in the Forest and the Eagle districts, then visited the Duomo (Siena's cathedral), where they were so thirsty from their exertions that we had to stop to buy more Diet Coke. This time they drank it during the walk, which continued without further pause through the most charming areas of the Panther, Snail, and Turtle districts.

At the heavy clang of bells sounding from the Mangia Tower, I realized that it was now time for lunch. My mouth began watering at the prospect of my friend Nello's *pici al tartufo*, which I certainly intended to order, until Mr. Franklin said in a serious, if not grave, tone, "Dario, I'm sorry, but in Italy you just don't know how to cook Italian food. You get the best genuine Italian food in America, so if you don't mind we'd prefer to eat over there." I followed the direction of his finger with growing consternation—till it led my gaze smack into the golden arches of McDonald's.

Having seen that they were people with a sense of humor, I thought they were pulling my leg; but no. They were utterly serious and utterly unmovable. Italians didn't know how to cook Italian food, so we'd be better off just going to McDonald's. Every attempt to make them change their mind, to give the Italians a chance, was useless. On this issue they had wills of iron. In a trembling voice I telephoned that fine restaurant, Da Nello, and canceled my reservation. And then, with my head hung low, I, an Italian, followed my American clients toward their inglorious fast-food temple. I felt alien and uncomfortable. Amid the neon lights, the plastic tables, the cardboard containers, nothing whatsoever called to mind a place where we might dine in peace.

To make it even worse, a group of noisy children was celebrating a friend's birthday, and a ridiculous clown cavorted among them, distributing balloons and paper party hats. I excused myself for a moment and retreated to the relative peace of the men's room.

Before returning I stopped to observe the Franklins from

behind the restroom door. Despite the circumstances, I couldn't help smiling at the sight of this middle-aged couple in their pastel gym suits, perfectly integrated into the rowdy fast-food atmosphere, contentedly stuffing themselves with french fries and hamburgers and downing everything with liters and liters of Diet Coke. They wore paper hats, and tied to their chairs were a pair of balloons with the unmistakable arched M waving forlornly above their heads. When we left they were very happy to receive as a gift some plastic toy hero from the next Walt Disney cartoon. As souvenirs of Siena go, this was unique in my experience.

Having left the Dragon district, we entered the Goose and the Owl, then stopped in a bar where the Franklins wolfed down their PowerBars and had an ice-cold Diet Coke each. We passed through the Giraffe, came down the steep street in the Caterpillar, then scrambled up the hard slope to the She-wolf without pause or complaint, until at last we arrived in the Porcupine. We had walked through all seventeen districts and thus reached our goal, so we returned to the hotel.

I took them to the TV room, where I showed them a video about the Palio, the bareback horse race around the Piazza del Campo that is the centerpiece of Siena's social and cultural year. They watched avidly as they snacked on a bag of potato chips (roast beef flavor) and more Diet Coke. During the screening we were briefly interrupted by a telephone call from their daughter, to whom Mrs. Franklin, without any embarrassment despite my presence, communicated her impressions of the day: "Siena is a really beautiful city, but it's all uphill and the restaurants don't serve real Italian food." And then she added, "Oh, and guess what; at McDonald's they even serve beer! Incredible, huh?" *Yes,* I thought: *incredible.*

I've maintained good relations with the Franklins, and they in return have sent many friends and relatives to tour with me. Eventually I also had the honor of accompanying their daughter. When I arrived to fetch her at the station in Florence, it was easy enough to pick her out of the teeming crowd: She was wearing a pale pink track suit and had a gigantic grin stretched across her face.

CHIANTI AND "CHIANTI"

If two diagonal lines were traced across the Italian peninsula—the first from Sicily to Austria, the next from Brindisi to Aosta—the center of this enormous X would be Tuscany. More precisely, and most appropriately, it would be Chianti. Just as Tuscany has been called the garden of Europe, so Chianti must be considered the garden of Tuscany.

For most people the name *Chianti* evokes simply the popular wine—though connoisseurs are aware that this unparalleled brew, this nectar of Bacchus, takes its name from its territory of origin, and not vice versa.

Actually, the truth about the two Chiantis is a bit more complicated (isn't it always?). Only the grapes grown in one well-defined and scrupulously regulated zone can produce the vintage called Chianti Classico. Other Chiantis produced in surrounding areas are often erroneously—if conveniently—confused with authentic Chianti.

Geographically, Chianti is a small area—just 200,000 acres—delineated on the east and west by fluvial borders, and to the north and south by the cities of Florence and Siena. The landscape is famously hilly. In the higher zones, which can climb to 1,800 feet, the landscape has volcanic origins, while in the lower valleys, once lapped by the waves of the Tyrrhenian Sea, the soil is sandy and rich in marine fossils. This patchwork geological constitution has made the cultivation of extensive crops nearly impossible—which explains why today, some 80 percent of Chianti is still blanketed by forests of chestnut and oak, and rare cypress groves.

The only crop that prospers in this rocky, barren land is the vine. In fact, the discovery of fossilized remains of *Vitis vinifera* (the ancestor of the modern grape) proves that the presence of this plant long predates the arrival of humankind. Of course, it took humans to fulfill the vine's divine destiny!

As early as the Etruscan period, wine was playing a major role in the area's economy. In more recent times olive production and limited cultivations in the south have been successful enough to give Chianti some agricultural diversity. Still, wine remains the undisputed king.

The asperity of the land has influenced the life of the area for centuries. Surviving on olives and wine is impossible, and growing the necessary additional crops is hugely difficult in the unyielding soil. For this reason Chianti has always been a region with a low-density population and very high poverty rates. The life of peasant sharecroppers in the nineteenth and early twentieth centuries was likely not very different from that of their medieval ancestors. I can imagine the local families gathering around the fireplace in their cold, damp stone houses and parceling out the small amounts of fruit they'd eked from the land—with a full half of the harvest being set aside for the demanding landowners.

In the late twentieth century, when Italy went through its postwar industrialization period, Chianti, like many other rural regions, suffered a near-total abandonment by its inhabitants.

The positive result of this migration was that Chianti remained largely immune to the architectural monstrosities that seemed to spring up all over the world at that time.

These days industrialization has yielded its primacy in Italian commerce to the old champion, tourism. And thanks to severe laws protecting the region's integrity, Chianti is enjoying something of a renaissance, as its splendid landscapes, uncontaminated resources, and architectural purity become ever rarer in the industrialized Western world.

Truly, a place worth raising a glass to!

FEBRUARY AND THE HONEYMOONERS

True, the weather can be miserable. But it can also offer ideal, limpid days on which to take long walks on the hills and take in the panorama of distant, usually invisible snowy mountain peaks. The song of the skylark may greet you, but you're unlikely to meet a fellow human being. You might, however, encounter a wild boar that dashes without warning from the bushes. There are also brownish hares, and multicolored pheasants so fat and torpid they seem easy enough to catch . . . though my dog has never managed it. Whenever he gets within striking distance, the birds become rattled and, incredibly, somehow contrive to take wing.

In the empty forests the first primroses and violets manage to pop out from the thick layer of rotting leaves. All is still, firm, and silent. It seems incredible that in just a few weeks, spring will burst forth here, with all its riot of color and quivering life.

February is the month in which I work the least, and I often take advantage of this dead period to go on vacation, visit some exotic country, and get my fill of beaches, rest, and sunshine. When I return my days at home are very quiet, the rhythm of life slow and steady. Finally I have time to relax, reflect, and make my plans for the coming season. In the morning, when the alarm clock rings, I know it's not for me but for Cristina, whose life continues at its usual pace; I can stay a while longer under the warm blankets and read, then roll out of bed and tend to daily rituals without hurry. Outside the window I can see that nature, lazier than me, is still asleep.

I think how my life has changed since I became a guide, how more and more my internal rhythms reflect those of the surrounding countryside. In winter we both retreat into a kind of hibernation in order to regenerate our energies for the challenges that await us. Spring awakens us gradually but soon forces us to recommence our work, inspiring us every day to produce more. In summer we will both be active and fruitful, nature with its bounty of crops, me with my bounty of overseas visitors. In autumn we begin to tire; the first leaves fall, and the summer abundance ends. But the soil of Chianti chooses this moment to bring forth its two best yields: grapes and olives—a final flurry of activity for both Mother Nature and myself. After the grape harvest the tourist season ends, leaving me time to pursue, step by careful step (from the picking to the bottling), the production of my own brand of extra-virgin olive oil.

In February there is sometimes snow, and the sight of the hills covered in sugared white is spectacular. Silence reigns then, becoming lord of the countryside. Everything comes to a halt—including, occasionally, the flow of electricity, with all its frustrating consequences: no light, no heat, no warm water, or no water at all if the pipes should freeze (as happens all too often). If snow falls in abundance, it's not uncommon to find yourself isolated in areas where the local councils aren't equipped to handle such natural phenomena. This can happen as often as twice a year. As a result, a few snowflakes are enough to put the whole community into a panic. Roads become impassable, public services stop functioning, and entire villages seem to come unmoored from civilization. But we all know that the following day the temperature may rise and melt the snow, bringing life back to normal. I have never loved snow much, except as a child when it prevented me going to school, and even now I prefer observing it from far away, as it glitters like diamonds on far-away mountain summits.

The village closest to my house is Vagliagli (which translates as "valley of garlic"), a graceful hamlet perched on a hill approximately 2.5 miles away. Its origins, as is the case for many villages of Chianti, is lost in the mists of time. Probably once an Etruscan settlement, it became a Roman colony, then in the Middle Ages was fortified for use as an outpost under the dominion of some powerful local family. To make it impenetrable during the many conflicts of that era, towers and imposing walls were erected; at the end of the wars in the sixteenth century, these were transformed into homes. Since it is not situated near any important road, Vagliagli has remained a bit cut off from the busy world, with the result that the population has dropped drastically. Today it has approximately 400 inhabitants.

Apart from a church and a square with a little bar, the village boasts two groceries, a restaurant, a post office, a wine bar that opens only during the tourist season, and a pharmacy that opens twice a week. The post office is the place I prefer, a very small site where everything has remained exactly as it was fifty years ago. The clerk, who boldly smokes like a chimney in full sight of the NO SMOKING sign, is a pleasant middle-aged woman who does all the work by hand, since computers are still very far from arriving to help her. The post office is nearly always empty except for the day the pension checks arrive; then Vagliagli's old people form a long line that, due to the building's tiny dimensions, must extend outside the door into the street. Incredibly, none of these pensioners trusts to have his money wired to his bank account. Each prefers to receive it by hand, then race over to the bank to deposit it.

The main grocery of the village is close to the public square, adjacent to the bar. It's a modern, functional store, well stocked, in which newspapers can also be purchased. The other grocery, on the ground floor of an old house, is an old-style shop that sells fresh vegetables grown in the local gardens. You can be served at every hour by ringing the bell, since the proprietors live upstairs. In high season the restaurant serves tourists above all, though it also has a following among the locals. The wine bar, managed by two young people from Siena, opens for dinner and is an alternative spot, where apart from tasting some good wines it's possible to eat the tasty snacks prepared by friendly Ghiga until late at night.

With the rise of the automobile in the 1960s, the butcher, the barber, the milk shop, and many other establishments vanished, since their wares were readily available in nearby Siena. But the social center of the village remains the bar, a typical Italian family operation richly supplied with liqueurs, digestives, fruit juices, fresh drinks, pastries, sandwiches, chocolates, candies, and of course coffee. On the second floor is a room where the seasoned old men gather to play cards, smoke, and discuss the next grape harvest over a drink. On the ground floor their women sit sipping coffee, chatting amiably, and trading gossip with the owner.

Whenever I visit these bars, I find myself newly fascinated by the variety of different coffees that customers can order. The classic espresso can be long or concentrated, splashed with warm or cold milk, high or low, flavored with a drop of liqueur, decaffeinated, and so on—and this is *before* considering the equally numerous variations on cappuccino. These can put even the most expert bartenders on the spot, because in Italy his skill is measured in part by his ability to remember the preferences of his frequent visitors, and to prepare the "usual" without requiring more explicit instructions.

With the arrival of foreigners, two new terms have appeared: *caffé americano*, to indicate the longer brew demanded from tourists unaccustomed to the tiny, concentrated, very strong Italian *caffé espresso*; and *latte*, which has come to refer to warm milk and coffee after numerous American visitors, using this word to order such a combination, instead found themselves confronted with a nice, cold glass of milk.

During the winter I often pass the time seated around the small tables of the bar drinking a *goccetto* and chatting with the old people; I enjoy hearing them rattle off stories of the past, or watching them rise to anger and even obscenity when a companion puts down an inconvenient card.

For me the company of the elderly is not unusual, as the greater part of my customers are what Americans call "seniors." But the old folks of Vagliagli are very different from the ones I escort around Chianti. They would never dream of undertaking overseas travel, renting a house, or adventuring with a rental car in a foreign country where they don't speak the language. For them, a day trip to Rome in a bus, organized by the parish priest, already represents a cause for significant agitation; imagine their distress should they be faced with boarding an airplane! When I see them seated at small tables, drinking and smoking and moaning about the government, I cannot help thinking of my Memphis clients, perhaps the most dynamic and adventurous I've ever known.

My association with them began courtesy of another of my clients, a Memphis preacher who was sufficiently impressed with the day I organized for him that he promised to send his flock my way. And sure enough, after his return to the States, my ratio of visitors from Memphis increased exponentially. I began to wonder whether, during his sermons, he was intimating to his faithful that time spent in Chianti with Dario was in the nature of a mystical experience (or perhaps a kind of atonement). However the word spread, it resulted a strange phenomenon: Virtually all the tourists who came to see me from Memphis were . . . well, elderly. Even today, when I accept a reservation from that city, I know what I'll find awaiting me at our rendezvous point: a group of smiling seniors, oozing friendliness and charm in a way Americans from the North seldom do, and greeting me with that lilting southern accent that I find so musical and pleasant.

In my years as a guide, I have had many clients who were in really bad shape—some using canes or wheelchairs, others deaf and arteriosclerotic, even those who were aware that this was probably their final trip. Nevertheless these people are almost invariably more amenable than many younger tourists and never display any intention to give up at any stage of the tour. I will never forget a tourist who only had one leg, who stubbornly and without accepting any help scrambled on his crutches up a muddy hill on a rainy day to see some excavated Etruscan tombs. I often ask myself whether it's recklessness or courage that pushes them to choose this rather complicated and laborious type of vacation. They seem to relish the difficulties, reserving remote country houses, renting manual-transmission cars, shopping on their own, cooking for and cleaning up after themselves, and then throwing themselves, virtually blindfolded, into long excursions with me, into territories they know nothing of and whose language they don't speak. Their utter trust and dependence on me is always surprising. After having spent a day with them, I can't but wonder how they manage to survive all these difficulties. In listening to their stories, though, I realize that in some way or another they not only survive but actually flourish, visiting all the important sites, finding the better restaurants, and enjoying their stay as fully as, if not more than, my able-bodied clients.

Of all my Memphis tour groups, however, one in particular encompassed all the phenomena that I've come to associate with my elderly clients.

On that particular morning I got up earlier than usual, since the address my clients had supplied me was unfamiliar and I realized I would have a task locating it. They had rented a beautiful country house in an equally splendid location, but so far out of the way that to find it they, not even being Tuscan, must have gone half mad. I parked my van and approached a deck chair that from behind appeared occupied—presumably by someone taking in the first rays of sunshine and the green sprawl of the hills. As I approached, I spotted more clearly a bald head strafed with a few white hairs—obviously an older man, and therefore most likely one of my customers. When I'd come within a yard or so, I greeted him with a friendly *"Buongiorno."* He didn't as much as budge; I could see now that he was reading a book. *"Buongiorno!"* I repeated, upping the volume—still no answer. For the third attempt I walked around the chair and stopped in front of him. Seeing me, he startled: "Oh, you must be Dario," he said getting up with some difficulty and leaning on his walking stick. "Come on in, I'll introduce you to the rest of the gang."

While we made our way up the gravel path, I tried to break the ice: "Is this your first time in Italy?" Alas, once again he didn't reply. I repeated the question, adding rather alarmingly to the heft of my voice and thinking of what my poor throat would be reduced to by the end of the day.

He heard me, and replied, "Absolutely not! I was here with the marines in '43."

In the kitchen another three old folks were finishing breakfast. They were a man in a wheelchair; a woman who, to judge by her trembling hands, was afflicted with Parkinson's disease; and another bent over a cane, wearing a pair of glasses with lenses so thick I couldn't see her eyes. I realized that one was missing, and hoped that at least the last and final member might be in good condition. Then a man with a pronounced limp entered the kitchen to greet me. It took me only a few moments to realize that one of his legs was false.

Perfect, I thought, *average age eighty, none fit—where the hell am I going to take these people if they can't walk or hear or even see me?*

"Can we offer you a coffee?" they asked me while pouring an unidentifiable brown sludge into my cup. Seeing my astonished expression, they explained that the coffeepot must be broken because they hadn't been able to make a decent cup since they'd arrived. I later learned that, instead of filling the filter with coffee grounds, they'd stirred the water and grounds together in the interior of the machine and then been perplexed that the filter hadn't worked.

It became increasingly apparent that the poor lot had been in the house for a week, completely out of place and with no one looking after them. The owner had come only the first day to collect the rent and offer a few basic instructions in Italian, which they of course didn't understand. Since his departure, my clients had yet to see anyone else connected with the property. As soon as they heard me speaking fluently in English, they sat me down and bombarded me with all sorts of questions: "Dario, could you make this phone call for me?" . . . "Dario, please, what's it say on this label?" . . . "Dario, can you go with us to the pharmacy?"

After having resolved their domestic crises, made their phone calls, and supplied them with all required translations, I thought it was high time to leave; but one of them asked, "Dario, you've been so patient, would you do just one last thing and take a quick look at our rental car? It doesn't go very fast, the oil light keeps blinking, and when we drive we give off a big black cloud of smoke. We think something might be wrong." I have never been very good with engines, but I reassured them that if the car needed repairs I could easily find them a good mechanic. "Great, then let's see what you think," the gentleman in the wheelchair said happily as he sped toward the exit, followed immediately by all the others. Despite their various afflictions, they managed to move at a surprisingly fast clip.

Outside, in a garage made of bamboo sticks, I asked for the keys and went for a test drive. The Fiat they'd rented worked perfectly, no black plume exited from the exhaust pipe, and I couldn't see any red light on the panel. Perplexed, I returned and asked if the group's designated driver would please sit in my place and take me for a spin around the house. This turned out to be the man I'd met on the deck chair. He slid into the driver's seat and off we went. This time the car did indeed proceed slowly, with a black cloud billowing from the back, while a red light on the panel winked frantically. Within a few moments I was also aware of the stench of burned rubber.

I could see at once that he hadn't released the parking brake, and I had the impression that he had never done so. How far had they driven like this . . . ? And how long had it *taken* them? Alarmed at the risks they'd run, I showed them all the main controls and explained the correct use of the brake.

Having solved this problem—brilliantly, they thought—I led everyone over to my van and finally got the tour in motion. But no sooner had we reached the gate than the lady with the thick glasses had to go back to the house because she'd forgotten her heart tablets. Once she was back in her seat, I succeeded in driving all the way beyond the gate before the gentleman with the wooden leg realized that he'd left his camera on the kitchen table. I drove him back to the front door, and while we waited for him to come back the lady with the cane said, "I think I'll take advantage of the wait and visit the bathroom."

"Good idea," said the lady with Parkinson's disease. "If you wait for me I'll go, too." After half an hour more of various last-minute details, we were at long last on our way . . . but as soon as we hit the main road, the group asked if I would take them to the nearest drugstore. In the village the pharmacist stared at me in disbelief when I handed him the list of medicines required. This stop was succeeded by visits to the bank, the post office, and finally the bakery because someone had begun to feel hungry. And no wonder—it was now lunchtime. And I still hadn't had a chance to start the actual tour.

We sat down to eat, and for the first time I noticed that they were all dressed similarly: the men with canvas fishing hats, horizontal-striped sailor shirts, pastel cotton pants, and Nike sneakers, the women in rather sober yet casual outfits clearly chosen for comfort—a far cry from some of my female clients, who come for a country tour lacquered with heavy makeup, wrapped in gaudy party clothes or animal-print pants and wearing high heels.

While we ate I tried to explain a bit of the history of the territory. Despite my efforts to project my voice, I had to repeat every thing two or three times. Finally giving in to the scarcity of their interest, I asked what, after all, was the purpose of their visit to Italy.

"It's our honeymoon!" they chimed.

"And Italy is such a romantic country," added the walking-stick lady.

At first I thought they were kidding, but they were utterly serious: They'd been wed the previous week. And that wasn't all. The woman with Parkinson's disease, after having been married to the hearing-impaired man from the deck chair, had now married the man in the wheelchair, while her ex-husband had married the woman with the cane—his seventh wedding in all. It took me a while to sort through all the intriguing and rather alarming relationships among the five of them. (What the man with the wooden leg was doing there I still haven't figured out.)

After lunch, which they wolfed down to the last crumb, I took them to visit Castle Brolio. By sheer coincidence the two people with hearing problems sat at the back of my mini bus, so that everything I said had to be repeated by the people seated behind me to those seated behind them. Still, as soon as we arrived at the castle, I had to repeat everything I'd said all over again, in answer to questions like "Dario, where exactly are we?" and "How nice! But who built it?"—and then again, incredibly, "Dario, tell us about this place." After I'd thus related the history of the castle twice—three times including the initial run-through in the car—the man with the wooden leg pulled a videocamera from his backpack and asked if I could repeat it once again so that he might put it on tape. Steeling myself, I began to tell the story of the castle for the fourth time; but when I had nearly finished, this amateur Spielberg realized he'd forgotten to insert a cassette. Fortunately neither of us had the stamina for a fifth performance. He simply turned off the machine.

Midway through the visit they started again to bombard me with questions, always the same ones, as if they'd completely forgotten the narrative I'd just related to them four times. I felt like a schoolteacher with a class of distracted pupils—but while the teacher can raise his voice and demand greater attention, I could only smile and endure it. (Besides which, I could scarcely raise my voice beyond the point I'd already pitched it.)

It began to feel uncannily like Chinese water torture. Immediately after my having said (again) that the castle of Brolio is property of the Ricasoli family, the deaf gentleman asked, "Dario, who does this castle belong to?"

Summoning up all my reserves of patience, I replied, "To the Ricasolis." As one they echoed, "Ah! Ricasoli."

"No," I corrected them, "not Ricasoli, but Ricasoli, with the accent on the *a*." At which point someone asked me for the spelling. "R-I-C-A-S-O-L-I," I replied.

"And what is the name of the castle of the Ricasoli?"

"Brolio," I answered for what seemed like the seventieth time.

"Brolio," she repeated thoughtfully. "Now, who does it belong to?"

"To the Ricasolis, an ancient Tuscany family," I replied in a voice that I am sorry to say was not without some trembling emotion in it.

"Ah, the Ricasolis," she said with a nod.

"Dario," interjected one of the men, "what did you say the name of the castle was? . . . Bettino, isn't that right?"

I took a deep breath. "Yes," I said, "the castle is called Bettino." He was going to forget it anyway.

Seeing that the group was climbing up the hill to the castle battlements with even less than their usual speed, I urged them to take it easy. I said I would go on ahead and wait for them at a spot where they could rest while taking in the breathtaking panoramic view—one of the most beautiful vistas in all Chianti.

For a while I lost myself in contemplation of the gently rolling hills, and it was only when I had become utterly relaxed that I realized my customers hadn't arrived yet. I backtracked to see what had happened to them. As soon as I turned a corner, I saw them encircling a woman who was stretched out on the ground. Immediately worried, I quickened my pace.

Soon I was close enough to see that the victim—with a deep cut on her forehead—was the lady with the cane and thick glasses. After 500 years of peace, the ancient castle walls were again being bathed in blood!

Fortunately she remained calm, and among the first rescuers on the scene was an American nurse on vacation. In her backpack, miraculously, she had a supply of disinfectant and bandages. A doctor, also vacationing, advised us to have the wound stitched, but once it was cleaned he could see that it was smaller than he'd feared and gave us his sanction to continue. Relieved but somewhat shaken, that's what we did.

The biggest fright, however, was still to come.

After the visit to the castle, of which everyone had already forgotten the name, I took the group to see an excavation of Etruscan tombs. In order to reach this place, we climbed a steep old Roman road—slightly daunting for my wheelchair-bound client, but with a little help he made it. It's a very pleasant wooded spot, especially in summer when the natural hedges of

Spanish broom are bright yellow and perfume the air with intense aroma.

In this short walk we met a viper. To be perfectly honest I don't ordinarily have any fear of this snake. Yes, it is potentially deadly, but in reality it's very timid and easily frightening by noise. It's an extreme rarity to encounter one in summer. If you do, it's usually on the asphalt roads, where they stop to absorb the heat radiating from the tar. In spring, when they come out of hibernation and are still sleepy and less reactive to noise, it's more common to come across them while putting your hands in some bush—or even unexpectedly treading on them while taking a walk. It's true that the bite of the viper is lethal, unless you make it to a hospital in time to have the antidote injected. In the thirty years I've lived in these hills, though, I've never heard of anyone being bitten.

Still, to prevent any unpleasant encounters—and also, I confess, to make a little show—every time I penetrate this rocky, bushy zone with my customers, I go ahead of the group and tap the ground, trying to make as much noise as possible to scare off any vipers. And on this day, with the happy gang behind me, I was doing exactly this when from behind me I heard one of the men call, "*Dariooo*—what is this *animal* on my foot?"

I turned around and was quite simply dumbstruck by what I saw. Between the legs of my eighty-year-old customer writhed a viper—about 8 inches long, gray speckled with black, with that unmistakable triangular head. Crossing the road, it had apparently come up against my client's foot. Having crawled over this obstacle, it now faced the other foot, and was making ready to crawl over that one in turn. Fortunately my client couldn't see very well, and couldn't distinguish exactly what it was that was coiling over his shoe.

"*Freeze,*" I ordered, managing to find my voice again. "Don't move a muscle!" And since I didn't want to alarm either him or the rest of the group, I told him he'd run across a rare example of a Chianti worm, an animal in danger of extinction that—according to an ancient legend—brings great fortune to anyone who comes in close contact with it. While I spun this improbable story, the viper slithered over the second foot and disappeared into the bushes. If the same thing had occurred to one of my younger customers, he no doubt would have died—if not from the bite, from the fright.

This group, however, was too limited in their perceptions to have been able to see exactly what had crept into their midst. Still, they were sharp enough to perceive that something of an ill nature had happened by the way in which I went pale as milk, and by my subsequent sigh of relief. It was only later, after having stopped for a drink, that I recovered from the shock and told them the truth.

During the return drive to their farmhouse, they all slept deeply. The passenger next to me supported his head on my shoulder and snored. I felt an urge to accelerate into the shoulder, pocked with potholes, and wake them all up, but this moment of perfidy passed quickly.

When I left them I felt, quite naturally, a sense of relief, but also to my surprise some genuine regret. Certainly they had been extremely difficult to manage, and no doubt had already forgotten every single thing I'd told them. But they'd treated me almost like a son; they had trusted me blindly, had willingly agreed to do whatever I proposed, and above all had never complained. And in their sense of adventure and sheer pleasure in being alive, they were in every way equal to the younger and more vigorous clients I've escorted through the wilds of Chianti.

CRADLE OF GENIUS

One attribute not in any way lacking in Tuscany is history. While it's possible to walk for hours without meeting another living soul, wherever you go you will find yourself surrounded by ghosts. All across our landscape still march the shades of the Etruscans, the uncanny race that sailed from somewhere in the Mediterranean and landed on our coasts about 700 B.C., changing forever the way of life here. Then of course there are the Romans, bringing us their great civilization in lock-step formation, constructing roads throughout Chianti that are still accessible today. And then there are the barbarians, almost literally swarming down from northern Europe, leaving in their wake formidable forts, towers, and, most lastingly, numerous descendants marked by their sharp Nordic features. On a quiet day, and with a fecund imagination, you can almost hear them all. Closing my eyes now, I imagine the battle cries of the Sienese and Florentine armies who periodically massacred each other over the epic centuries of civil war.

But the period of which we are proudest is the *Rinascimento*—the Renaissance—of which Tuscany was the cradle. After centuries of war, ignorance, disease, and superstition, there was born here a movement of profound philosophical, commercial, and cultural progress. Leonardo da Vinci, during his residence at a farm called Vignamaggio, painted the Mona Lisa. The Buonarroti family has its origins in Chianti, where it seems that these relatives of Michelangelo were winemakers.

Amerigo Vespucci, after whom the American continent is named, was the owner of a farm at Montefioralle, and his neighbor Giovanni from Verrazano owned the eponymous castle situated close to Greve in Chianti. I like to think these two great navigators found the inspiration for their oceanic achievements while contemplating the wavy, sea-green hills surrounding their properties.

Niccolò Machiavelli, a *chiantigiano* from birth, wrote *The Prince* in Sant'Andrea in Percussina, where it is still possible to visit the house in which he lived as a student and worked for many years. Galileo Galilei, who lived in Arcetri but possessed a small farm at Grignano in the heart of Chianti, often praised the product of his lands, boasting that his wine could leave all others in the dark. During the difficult years of his excommunication, he sought solace in a house called La Torraccia as a guest of the Ricasolis.

I could continue this honor roll of Renaissance titans—but to name all the artists and thinkers who came here to seek inspiration, or create timeless masterworks, would require more space than the theme of this book allows.

In subsequent centuries Chianti again fell many times beneath the warrior's boot. Our fields provided passage to Napoleonic troops. They served as a theater in the wars of Italian independence (from which a local hero arose, another member of the Ricasoli family: the powerful Iron Baron, Bettino).

It is certainly difficult today, amid the serenity bred by these sweet hills, to imagine the awesome tragedy of the First World War, from which thousands of young local men never returned. It is equally difficult to conjure up the fear and horror of the German occupation of World War II, or the heroic Resistance movement that hid in the local forests until the liberation by the Allies—who on their way north again marched over our fragile fields with their massed troops, powerful artillery, and tanks. As a testament to those sad years, every village in Chianti has a monument carved with the names of its victims, martyrs, and heroes.

And today? . . . Today Chianti should be admired and preserved as a repository of natural and cultural beauty. Strangely, this seems to be occurring, thanks less to the energies of our natives than to the enthusiasm of tourists and expatriates. The wealth they have brought to the area has contributed dramatically to a second *rinascimento*. As I have noted, ancient farmhouses have been lovingly restored while wild building speculation is practically nonexistent, and virtually all our small villages have restored public squares and roads, resurrecting their value and fascination as medieval artifacts.

The greater number of our farms are now the property of foreigners, because it was these nonlocals who were the first to see the advantages and the potential of this wonderful land. For this phenomenon many *chiantigiani* hold a grudge. I, however, believe that anyone who loves this territory is entitled to live here, on the condition that he or she respects the place and its traditions and contributes to the maintenance of our historical and natural patrimony. On these terms Chianti waits for you, too—whether for a visit of a few hours, a weekend, a month, or perhaps the rest of your life. A sufficient time period to render justice to the beauties of this region does not exist.

MARCH AND THE OENOPHILE

N ow come violent winds that sweep away the fallen leaves, and for a short time the countryside lies naked. It seems to me a ritual purge that precedes the eruption of spring. The sun suddenly remembers how to warm the ground, and the snakes emerge from a long sleep. Still half dormant, they lie basking in the fields. Even the venomous viper seems to pose no threat as it dozes, happy and defenseless. Its nonlethal relatives, often alarmingly large, can be glimpsed as they slip lazily through the bushes, their bold black-and-yellow markings disguising the fact that they are actually gentle, even lovable creatures.

In March the lizards reappear. The first spring flowers timidly come into view: violets, primroses, wild narcissi, forest anemones, and everywhere peach and apricot trees, and wild prunes. The garden fills with sparrows and tits, some busy building nests in the cracks of the old walls, others restoring the ones abandoned in autumn. Easter is approaching and the old parish priest, carrying sacred incense and trailed by small boys, goes door to door for the customary annual blessing.

In March I also come out of hibernation and find myself increasingly inundated by reservations and excursions. Once again my everyday routine becomes: wake up, collect clients, spend the day touring. The days fill quickly, both with sights and sounds, and with new faces.

It was in March that I made the acquaintance of TT. He contacted me for the first time in January 1993. I came home one afternoon and found that my fax machine had spat out a long sheet of paper on which a prospective client had listed a seemingly infinite series of questions and requests. I immediately noticed the great interest this man had in wine—much more than just a hobby, judging from the list of vineyards he wished to visit.

There were so many that in order to satisfy him, I would have had to take him out daily for more than a month.

Thus began a long correspondence between us. To every fax filled with questions that arrived, I sent back an equally long response. He would read it seemingly immediately and fax me again with further requests and demands, and always questions upon questions. Every time I recommended a hotel or restaurant, he wanted to know more about it. The first such requests were understandable—he wanted to clarify the hotel's location, services offered, type of food served, what have you. But then, after having provided this information, I would receive additional and, I thought, incredible questions regarding the dimensions in square feet of the hotel rooms and baths, the height of the ceilings, the presence or absence of wallpaper, the color of the walls, and so on.

Day after day the correspondence continued, growing increasingly bizarre. Finally, after two months of negotiations and fifty-one faxes, we established that we would meet on March 19 at his hotel on the outskirts of Siena and tour the area's vineyards, tasting as many wines as possible, omitting every aspect of the territory that wasn't connected to anything oenological.

Despite our immense correspondence I had no picture of this man in my head; he had revealed nothing about himself to help me form one. But I was so curious to meet him that the night before his arrival I actually dreamed about him. In these dreams he was a tiny, nervous man, very distinguished and demanding, difficult to satisfy, quick to complain. He also kept ordering me to do things without giving me the time to do them, and repeatedly asked me questions that had no answers because he enjoyed making me feel uncomfortable. I woke up in a sweat, my throat dry and my lips parched. Was it possible that the coming meeting with TT had caused me so much stress? Or were the nightmares due to the spicy pizza I had downed with perhaps too much red wine the night before? I got out of bed and drank almost a liter of water, remembering the adage "What doesn't die with wine will drown in water." It was only four o'clock; there were still six hours to my appointment. I returned to bed. In the morning I woke up with a light headache and a small kernel of fear. I went to collect TT at the expensive five-star hotel where he had reserved a suite.

He was waiting for me, seated on the couch in the lobby, puffing on a cigarette. He was enormous; his body made me think of an American football player—one who after ending his career had packed on some excess pounds. Long, uncombed brown hair fell down around his shoulders. His gigantic biceps seemed ready to rip through his shirt sleeves, and his chest was so large it seemed capable of absorbing all the oxygen in the room in a single gulp. His belly was big—not in a sloppy, dangle-over-the-belt-buckle way, but large and compact, as if he were on the point of giving birth to twins. His knees had the circumference of soup bowls.

The concierge alerted him of my arrival and he rose—and

rose—and rose—till he was standing at well over 6 feet. Then with slow, heavy movements he approached me. The collection of porcelain on the hotel mantel trembled. I swallowed nervously.

"Dario, pleased to meet you," he said, crushing my hand as if it were an orange in a juice maker. To break the ice, I looked up and said, "So what's the weather like up there?" His face lit up, and he burst into friendly, booming laughter—again putting at risk the precious porcelain.

As he got into the car, I realized that the image I had formed of him could not have been more wrong. I found myself in company of a pleasant, overgrown boy, accommodating and very easygoing. It seemed impossible that the person sitting next to me was the manic correspondent with whom I had traded so many frantic faxes.

But TT did have a mania: wine. His was a real passion; he knew every single vintage, all the grape varieties, the different vinification techniques, even the types of bottles. When we sat at a table and ordered a wine, he always wanted it decanted and served in the glasses best suited to it, because for him wine was something sacred. In my many years at this job, I have met quite a few wine nuts, but nobody has held a candle to TT. As soon as a bottle was opened, he began his ritual. First he analyzed the cork; after the wine was poured into the decanter, he would smell it, nearly inhaling it; once it was poured for us, he observed the color while turning the goblet toward the light. Then, lowering his head and inserting his nose, with his cheekbones supported on the goblet's rim, he remained fixed for entire minutes to prevent even one tiny scented molecule from escaping him.

After this first phase he commenced the tasting. He captured the first drop with the tip of his tongue, where the papillae are more sensitive, then pursed his lips and somehow made them vibrate, emitting a sound similar to the snarl of a cat. Next he returned to an upright position and sipped, always slowly rotating the glass between sips with an emphatic turn of his hand.

After emptying the glass he gave his verdict—which was never restricted to the usual judgments of *rough* or *full-bodied* or *drinkable*. No, TT's repertoire of diagnoses included *sweetish*, *acetous*, *dry*, *wide*, *aristocratic*, *aromatic*, *acidulous*, *acrid*, *acute*, *adulterated*, *acid*, *aggressive*, *sour*, *altered*, *amiable*, *bitter*, *astringent*, *austere*, *shining*, *burning*, *burned*, *butyric*, *warm*, *tarlike*, *short*, *cooked*, *decrepit*, *delicate*, *defective*, *disharmonious*, *sweet*, *sweetish*, *hard*, *effervescent*, *balanced*, *herbaceous*, *eternal*, *frank*, *thin*, *seasoned*, *structured*, *tasty*, *velveteen*, *winish*, *lively*, *alive*, *foxy*, and *hairy* (?!). The description of the colors and the different types of fruit that he could distinguish at every sip involved another long list of adjectives that I will, in the interest of momentum, spare you.

TT had drunk wine for decades, but this was his first visit to Tuscany and thus his first opportunity to see the wineries and vineyards that until now he had only read about. At every stop it was like taking a child to a chocolate factory. Often I saw him grow deeply emotional while he was introduced to the most famous producers and winemakers of the area—people who to him had heretofore existed on some almost mythological plane. Each time, his eyes filled with delight, he would radiate enthusiasm while he crushed hand after hand.

One thing that shocked me was his apparently inexhaustible financial resources. In restaurants he invariably ordered the most expensive wines on the list, forcing the alarmed restaurateurs to uncork bottles of priceless vintages they'd kept locked in the cellar for years. At the end of every meal, he was presented with an astronomical bill that he not only paid without comment but also supplemented with a tip worthy of a sultan. And since he obviously enjoyed my company, he insisted on buying me a bottle of every wine I had shown any enthusiasm for. Of course I put forth polite protestations, but he overruled them with a wave of his hand, so that each night I returned home with several new bottles to add to my collection.

One day in Montalcino, he rendered me speechless by purchasing a bottle worth many millions of *lire*. That evening when we returned to his hotel, he asked me to carry it up to his room while he dealt with some private matter at the desk. Pretending to be calm, I said, "Sure, TT, no problem." But when I started climbing the stairs, I felt my legs grow more wobbly with each step. The last flight was the most difficult—it seemed endless— and as I breathlessly gripped the bottle, I tried to dispel from my mind an image of me crying over a heap of broken glass, its priceless contents seeping into a Persian rug. Fortunately all went well; the bottle is now resting with 55,000 counterparts in the private underground cellar of TT's Florida villa.

On our last day together, now that we had become fast friends and were in perfect concord, I confessed to him that after all those faxes that I'd received in January, I was expecting to meet a very different person, more meticulous and above all less friendly and jovial. TT started laughing, which made the entire car quiver slightly. "With all the business I have to conduct in Florida," he explained, "I don't have time to organize my vacations myself." It turns out my faxed correspondence had not been with him, but with his secretary. His very *thorough* secretary.

It was a beautiful spring day, and thus we decided to pay a visit to my friend Paolo, owner of a small farm in the Chianti Classico hills. My tiny cross-country vehicle scrabbled up a steep, rocky road bordered on each side by olive trees. When we arrived we parked in front of Paolo's beautiful fifteenth-century colonial stone farmhouse. Three rather warlike geese came hissing at us, but once they saw that we weren't the least intimidated, they backed off. The cellar was unlocked, and we entered through its tiny, dank doorway, which was surmounted by an impressive vine that was showing its first slender shoots.

There was no trace of Paolo. Then I heard someone call my name. I couldn't figure out where it came from until I saw a hand extending from the small opening in one of the five 9,000-liter oaken barrels aligned against the cellar wall. "I'm over here!" cried Paolo. TT seemed astonished that a human being could fit into such a tight space, and hastily searched his pockets for his camera in order to immortalize this unusual sight.

It really did seem uncanny that a grown man could fit himself through such a narrow opening, but as Paolo said with a shrug, "If the head passes, so can the rest of the body." Looking at the gigantic TT, I decided that perhaps this theory wasn't true in all cases.

Once outside Paolo took off his overalls, put on his spectacles, and in the space of an "Amen" changed his image from worker to owner. He took an old straw *fiasco* and filled it with wine. "This," he said, "is a preview of my next reserve. And this," cutting into a little wheel of cheese on the mantelpiece, "the best-seasoned pecorino in Chianti. Here is bread baked today by my wife, Gianna, in the old firewood oven. And last but not least, I'll go and fetch some fresh fava beans from my vegetable garden." Thus, with a bite of cheese, one of *fave*, and a *gotto* of wine, we sat ourselves beneath an ancient mulberry tree and spoke of the only subject dear to TT: wine.

"You see," Paolo explained in his colorful English (even

more incomprehensible with his mouth full), "all my property is encircled by grapevines. But until fifty years ago, in this house where my wife and two sons and I now live, there were perhaps twenty people, and on this land they had to cultivate everything they needed in order to be self-sufficient. The wine that is for me my sole source of income was for them just a small percentage of the crops they farmed—although it was very important to them, since in the winter wine was their only source of vitamin C. Therefore they considered it more than a drink, a true food. It was normally consumed young for the same reason: In aging, wine loses many of its beneficial properties. In fact, there's a well-known peasant saying—'Bread of a day, wine of a year, and a woman of twenty.'"

TT listened intently to these stories and asked innumerable questions. When he asked why white grapes were added in small amounts to the original Chiantis, Paolo, throwing back his third glass, told us that this was done to keep the alcohol rate lower, since children had to drink the wine as well. He recalled that when he was a boy, his mother would serve him bread dipped in wine with some sugar on top for breakfast. The Ricasoli baron who dictated the rules of Chianti wine production in the nineteenth century really only imposed the percentages of grapes already used by the peasants (80 percent Sangiovese and 10 percent Canaiolo Nero, both red, plus 5 percent each Trebbiano Toscano and Malvasia del Chianti, both white). It was for this reason Chianti became so popular; it was the people's everyday wine.

As its success spread throughout the world, cheap table wines produced virtually everywhere started adopting the name *Chianti*. Fortunately, as I explained to TT, we imposed strict rules to guard the genuine product, and today Chianti can only be produced in designated zones of Tuscany, while Chianti Classico is produced only in the actual Chianti region.

We continued talking for several hours, blissfully unaware of the time. TT, who was obviously very happy to have met this small, witty, proud entrepreneur, asked why here in our hills we still use the traditional straw-covered bottle. I explained that the bottles were once mouth-blown, so that the bottoms were often irregular and therefore wouldn't stand upright on the table. This was the origin of the word *fiasco*. Tradition holds (goodness knows if it's true) that Leonardo da Vinci himself came up with the reed support. The basket also kept the wine cool and fresh when the farmers brought the container into the fields on torrid summer days.

In the 1960s *fiasco* bottles became popular for their ornamental value. Certain producers, noticing that people purchased them less for their contents than to use as candleholders later, began filling the *fiascoes* with minor-quality wines. Which is why, TT added, deducing this though a bit tipsy, the *fiasco* became synonymous with *cheap wine*.

As the sun was setting behind Monte San Michele, we finally decided to leave Paolo, who insisted that I take half a suckling pig he had roasted in the oven. A bit embarrassed by his largesse, I accepted the gift, which he'd hastily wrapped in paper, and put it in the backseat of my van. Paolo slipped into his work clothes again and went back inside the barrel, and TT and I headed back to Siena. I seemed to be driving with greater difficulty than usual, and it occurred to me to consider the amount of wine I had imbibed.

In the distance I saw a *carabinieri* roadblock, and I

explained to TT that this was nothing more than a routine check. They waved a little red placard in front of me, and I stopped on the side of the road.

"Good evening," said the young officer in his elegant Armani uniform. "May I see your license and car documents, please?" While they examined the documents, I urged TT not to worry, that this was a simple formality, even though a machine gun was pointed in our direction. I also explained to him that in Italy, the *carabinieri* police are much loved though much mocked, and that many jokes are made about them because their ranks are traditionally filled by simple people from the south.

When the young officer handed back my documents, he politely asked what I was transporting on the backseat. "Half a pig," I answered.

"I see." A pause. "Is it dead or alive, sir?"

I choked back a laugh that would have betrayed my state of light inebriation. "Dead," I answered in a grave voice.

"Okay. Have a nice trip. *Buonasera.*"

As soon as we were on the road, I translated the officer's questions for TT, and he burst into laughter. He had now had a firsthand illustration of why we tease the *carabinieri* so much.

We returned safe and sound to the hotel despite 20 miles of bends and turns.

I remained in contact with TT; nearly every year thereafter he returned, and we went from vineyard to vineyard, drinking scores of wines. Often, between visits, he phoned to ask me for information on the new vintages.

Just a short time ago, however, he called to tell me that he had been diagnosed with a serious form of diabetes and wasn't allowed to drink wine any longer. This is almost certainly the worst thing that could have happened to him.

FOSCO'S HOUSE

Despite my rebellious teenage style (long dyed hair, earrings, shirttails worn outside my torn jeans, clumsy paratrooper boots), I managed to make friends with some of the old men of the village. Perhaps they were actually attracted by my defiant bohemianism. One of these men was called Fosco.

Fosco Lolini was one of those genuine personalities who, once encountered, can never be forgotten. I met him one evening in his little open-air place. Here, beneath a bower of Mediterranean pine trees, he served on sunny days sandwiches stuffed with local hams and salamis, Tuscan wines, and occasionally (when in the right mood) some hot meals. He was a short fellow, a typically dark Etruscan type, despite his thick hair—once probably jet black—having gone snow white. I went often to eat at the Pinetina, hoping selfishly each time that I would be the only customer, because Fosco would then sit beside me and regale me with stories of my beloved Chianti. I liked it when he sat across from me, lowering his head so as to view me over the rims of his presbyter eyeglasses. He was very different from most of the old *chiantigiani* I had known, for Fosco retained an eager, open mind and had kept pace with the changing realities of our time. For this reason he served as a kind of link between the old peasant generation and their modern inheritors. Although he was mostly self-taught, he possessed an immense capacity for knowledge: He could recite by heart entire passages of Dante's *Commedia* as well as many other classics of Italian literature, and was a vocal admirer of Saint Augustine. I can never be sufficiently grateful to Fosco for all the time he devoted to me and for the things he taught me about peasant life.

One day he invited me to see the farmhouse where he had lived as a boy, and with great joy I accepted. We made the drive in his tiny, thirty-year-old Fiat 500—always as polished and bright as if it were brand new. Leaving the main road, he pulled onto a narrow, muddy path that had so rough a surface even a modern four-wheel-drive vehicle would have had trouble with it. After twenty bumpy minutes we came upon a clearing surrounded by brilliant bushes of yellow Spanish broom, and in the center stood a spectacular stone house. It was very large, comprising two floors with the classic turret in the center.

We parked the car in the abandoned chicken yard and climbed the dangerously weather-eaten stone steps that led to the main entrance, which sat beneath a pretty little porch that had a pair of large arch-shaped windows. A light push, and the old chestnut door creaked open. We entered.

We found ourselves in a hall dominated by an enormous hearth, large enough to accommodate two benches for those icy winter evenings when the peasants gathered there for warmth and conversation. The pavement, completely worn away by centuries of heavy tread, was no longer flat but wavy. Fosco was visibly moved as he pointed out where the great wooden table was once placed, where he'd sat with the other nineteen people who made up his family. He reminded me that in those years there was no electric light; water came from the well, which he now pointed out to me through an open window looking onto the courtyard. With his eyes misty, Fosco recalled long evenings passed in front of the flickering fire, roasting chestnuts and drinking red wine, while the women sewed and his grandfather told age-old stories with everyone listening in almost religious silence.

In each of the four corners of the main hall, there was a door. The first led to a room that had the wall adjacent to the fireplace; this being, obviously, the warmest room, it was where the older people slept. The door on the opposite side opened onto a long corridor off which four other rooms were accessed; these were where the children slept. To see them now, lying empty behind broken windows and immersed in an almost spectral silence, it was hard to believe that once they had been filled with voices, warmth, and an accumulation of family artifacts.

In that dusty desolation the only sign of life was a family of barn owls that had nested under the beams of the ceiling.

We retraced our steps and crossed to the third door, in the other wing of the house. Here again there were a few empty rooms, as well as a staircase that led up to the turret. The room at the top was used as a dovecote; it was also where the farmers here had jealously stored their precious *vin santo*, the sweet wine they broke out only on special occasions.

The last door off the main hall opened onto a descending staircase. Here the cobwebs were so thick that it was only with some difficulty that we made our way down to the large rooms just off a patio where the farmers kept their equipment. We were now in the deserted stables. At one time these would have been full of livestock and tools; now there remained only a few scattered bales of straw and wooden stacks. Out in the courtyard

Fosco pointed out the pigpen, a detached, low-lying construction set far apart from the rest of the house. He tried to give me a picture of the daily life on the farm: the chickens swarming all over the place, free to seek out their own food, the stables full of dairy cows, and all around the property little plots of vines, grains, vegetables, fruit trees. Despite the enormous difficulties, even a small farm could achieve self-sufficiency, producing everything it needed save for salt. Fosco said they even managed to extract sugar from the beets, and to raise silkworms by feeding them the fruits from two mulberry trees that were yet standing here.

I hadn't noticed any toilet, so I asked where it might be. Fosco smiled and pointed out a small hut with a tiny door, well outside the house. Curiosity compelled me to investigate. I pushed open the door; inside were two deformed wooden planks to support the feet, and a hole dug directly in the earth. When I recoiled from this rather spartan apparatus, I stumbled on an old leather shoe. Fosco picked it up and, after examining it, carefully deduced from its enormous size that it had belonged to his father. An old cart full of demijohn bottles covered with decades' worth of dust and dirt was leaning on an ancient wall— a wall built, in fact, in the 1500s.

What I thought was a pleasant discovery for my old friend seemed instead to bring back painful memories of the sufferings and privations of his peasant beginnings. "Dario," he said, opening his hands and showing me his callused palms, "you've surely noticed how people of my generation are bent and aged prematurely? Well, our life has been a tough one. We worked in the fields, sometimes for sixteen hours a day, trying to eke from this miserable, ungenerous Chianti soil whatever it was able to give us. We ate always the same things and never in abundance; I mean, we had next to nothing. Even worse, at the end of the month, the landowner arrived, and we sharecroppers were obliged to give him half our miserly crop. The closest village was 11 miles away, and obviously we couldn't afford a horse; so whenever there was a need for something, it was 'legs on shoulders'—off we went, walking for hours."

He paused, then added, "Come, I want to show you something." We followed a narrow path, now partially barricaded by overgrown bushes, that took us through a small forest of splendid cypresses—and abruptly came upon a tiny cemetery encircled by a high stone wall. We passed through the rusted gate. Before us lay about thirty nearly identical tombstones, most obscured by high grass. Observing the simple crosses, I noticed that most had engraved upon them Fosco's family name, and that the dates indicated many premature deaths. Moved, I turned to Fosco, wanting to tell him that I understood how difficult it must have been to survive in this type of world; but I saw that he had removed his hat and lowered his head, as if in prayer. I kept my peace. A little while later he ushered me away. We returned to the Fiat without saying a word.

After a few minutes' drive on the muddy side road, he broke the silence to indicate through the windshield a small monument in memory of some of his partisan friends, killed during the Second World War.

Back on the main road, we realized that we were hungry and so stopped at a trattoria. There, over a plate of homemade tagliatelle and a good honest *fiasco* of wine, Fosco told me that since the day he had left the farmhouse with his family in 1954, he had never returned to it—never found the courage to confront again the place where he had grown up amid so much hardship. Now he was happy to have done so.

Many years after the death of my beloved friend, I decided to return to his old house to relive that memorable day. But as I approached, I found that the road had been repaired; a large gate had been erected to prevent anyone from getting too close. Peering through its bars, I saw children diving into a swimming pool that had been dug next to the old courtyard and two shiny Mercedes Benzes with German plates parked in what was once the humble stable. There was even a satellite dish on the turret.

I shifted into reverse and backed away at full speed.

APRIL AND THE KNOW-IT-ALLS

Suddenly the countryside explodes in a majestic exuberance of wildflowers and foliage. True, it often rains, but in the face of such luxuriant flora, no one dares complain. The dogwood blooms and the beech trees enter that short but glorious season in which their leaves are an intense emerald green. Here and there in the budding forests, you'll find manna ash with clusters of creamy, fragrant buds; the whitethorn blossom is virtually everywhere, as is the wild cherry. Wisteria, lilacs, orchids, and hyacinths push their way through cracks on the walls along the road.

During rainfalls virtual armies of toads invade fields covered by carpets of primroses, and sometimes it's even possible to see a salamander. The ancients believed this creature could survive flame, a rather strange theory considering it lives only in the most humid zones. Its slow, deliberate movements make it look like a mechanical toy next to the ubiquitous lizards, which dart away in the wink of an eye, leaving an afterimage of their yellow specks like drops of paint in the sun. In these days, too, you can hear the first cuckoo sing. A local proverb maintains that if the song of the cuckoo isn't heard by the eighth of April, there will be death and disease within domestic walls.

On some spring nights a strong wind rises unexpectedly, and in the distance you can hear the unmistakable growl of thunder; then the storm rolls in and sends its deafening downpour onto the roof with the force of a shower jet turned on full blast. The windowpanes begin to rattle, and through the shutters the flash of lightning illuminates the room with the seizurelike cadence of a strobe light. It's not unusual that when these storms sweep in, electrical power shorts out. The only thing to do then is stand before the window and enjoy the show, listening to the thunder tumble over the valley and watching as the lightning throws the towns perched on the hills into momentary stark relief. Of these towns the most spectacular is surely San Gimignano, whose profusion of medieval towers pierce the stormlit sky even more dramatically than in daylight, when the haze can make them difficult to discern. Observing these architectural jewels from afar, I often wonder if my awe of them is due to their status as one of the most recognizable landmarks in Tuscany, or whether they really are sufficiently beautiful to be appreciated from a great distance.

The wind shrieks with increasing shrillness, yet my dog lies in a corner sleeping peacefully, very happy indeed to be inside rather than on one of his nocturnal forays through the forests. After about twenty minutes the storm rolls systematically south, the once deafening thunder now a mere echo from a distance, the jagged bolts of lightning reduced to the intensity of tourist flashbulbs. The cherry tree, already in blossom, stops waving to and fro, and its shadow, projected on the wall of the drawing room, relaxes like a dancer at the end of a fierce arabesque.

Before slipping beneath the blankets, I open the window and breathe in the ozone residue, its indescribable aroma a mixture of humid earth, fresh grass, and flowers in bloom. In bed I think about the next day, certain it will be a beautiful one. The morning after a rainstorm is usually limpid and gentle, with a sky that seems daubed into place by a paintbrush.

And so it is. Taking advantage of the glorious weather, Cristina and I have breakfast in the garden, surrounded by the hundreds of red poppies that have opened on the lawn haphazardly yet irresistibly, as in an impressionist painting.

The fresh air instills energy for the rest of the day, and as we breathe it in, we observe the first bees encircling the peach flowers that soon will give forth with ripe, sweet fruit.

It was on just such a splendid morning that I set off to meet a pair of new clients. I arrived at the Villa Scacciapensieri, a beautiful four-star hotel complex with a tongue-twisting name my Anglo-Saxon clients invariably have difficulty pronouncing. Many guests, evidently inspired by the magnificent day, were having breakfast outdoors beneath a colorful wisteria vine now in full, resplendent flower.

Bruce, the gigantic, red-haired concierge, received me as always with his curious Tosco-Scots accent: "Who are yuir customers today?" Someone named Taylor, I replied. He shot me a sly, amused look, and I understood that I would be dealing with some more-than-usually interesting people.

As is my custom, I waited for my clients in the lobby, sinking into one of the comfortable armchairs and leafing through the Siena paper. I reflected on the cleverness of the editors, who succeed in issuing a new edition every single day in a city where nothing actually happens.

My thorough reading of an article on the front page—about a domestic accident in which a woman cut her finger peeling a potato—was interrupted by the appearance of two strikingly beautiful women. Both were blond, statuesque, and had brilliant blue eyes. This physical similarity was echoed in their dress: Each wore pink sneakers, tight jeans, and a positively adhesive T-shirt that seemed woefully insufficient to the task of containing such ample breasts. At once I guessed them to be sisters, if not twins.

These must be the Taylors, I thought, without a trace of disappointment. This assumption was reinforced by their unmistakable New York accents, and by the fact that, with their backpacks slung over their shoulders and their cameras hung about their necks, they were obviously waiting to be taken on some kind of excursion.

I leapt from the couch and brightly said, "Hello, I'm Dario. Are you ready?" They nodded and smiled, displaying that most American of attributes: dazzling white teeth set in rows as even as piano keys. Quite content to be stuck with these two striking women for the day, I led them to my van. As soon as they climbed in, they asked how much time it would take to reach Rome.

"Rome?" I said, confused. "But . . . haven't you reserved a tour of Chianti?"

"Oh, no," they said. "We're waiting for a ride to the airport." I felt myself deflate slowly, like a punctured tire.

Glumly I led them back into the hotel, where Bruce, who had observed the scene, grinned evilly at my embarrassment, then nodded toward a couple just now stepping from the elevator.

He was a distinguished gentleman, about seventy, with a polished bald head set above a large pair of 1950s-style black-framed sunglasses. He wore a Ralph Lauren Polo shirt, General Rommel–style baggy shorts, bleached white socks pulled right up to the knees, and a pair of Clarks on his supersized feet.

She had a nest of blond, nearly white hair, a mouth somewhat deformed by phosphorescent pink lipstick, and a deep layer of powder spread across a face from which her eyes bulged alarmingly, thanks to the heaviest green mascara I had ever seen. She wore a shiny gold jacket over a black T-shirt stitched full of sequins and a pair of tight elastic leopard-print pants, which she had tucked into high-heeled black boots similar to those worn by Pussy Galore in that James Bond movie. Her appearance was rendered even more astonishing by a virtual jewelry store of authentic baubles—so large as to make them initially appear false—draped over her every available appendage, like the decorations on a Christmas tree.

Luckily I had phoned the day before and left word that they should dress casually. If I hadn't, God only knows how this woman would have shown up.

At that moment my more fortunate colleague pulled up in front of the hotel, and I watched as the two blond princesses climbed into his car and were carried away by him.

"Are you Dario?" The question brought me back to my genuine clients. I fleetingly considered answering in the negative, then nodded weakly, and they introduced themselves.

The tour began fairly well, except for a few small inconveniences. Mrs. Taylor's golden jacket and all those jewels were so blindingly brilliant under my open sunroof that I had no choice but to keep the rearview mirror turned aside. Also, each time we entered an inhabited area of any size, she insisted that we close the windows and lock the car doors—apparently out of fear that someone would attack the van and steal her glittering cargo.

On the path that leads to the Etruscan tombs, she was forced to remove a boot after the heel got wedged between two slabs of stone. At lunch she ate like a sparrow, but in compensation drained an entire liter of Diet Coke. From the restaurant's women's room, she summoned me three times—first because she couldn't find the light switch, then because she didn't know how to pull the flushing arm, and finally because she had somehow gotten locked inside. I must admit that in this final crisis I was sorely tempted to leave her trapped; had I but done so, I would have spared myself the unanticipated sight of her with her showgirl makeup "freshened," which I think removed some years from my life.

By far the strangest aspect of the tour—one for which I still have no explanation—was that Mrs. Taylor, knowing in advance that I was Italian, took it for granted that I couldn't understand her. And she was unwilling to abandon this preconception even after we had met. Despite my not only being fluent in English, but speaking it (so I am told) with a bourgeois British accent, Mrs. Taylor addressed me as though I were a child or someone mentally impaired. Every word was pronounced very slowly, accompanied by broad gestures. And thanks to all those jangly bracelets and bejeweled rings, each such gesture produced an annoying metallic racket and a volley of snapshot-like flashes.

At one point, while visiting a church, she—gesturing wildly— said, "Daario, we've seen so maany works of art by the same Italian faamily. In every city, in all the museeums and gaalleries, there are masterpieces by this same family from over the cennturies. How is it possible that one faamily could produce so many geeniuses?"

Although I'm fairly well versed in Italian art, I could think of no such dynasty, so I asked, "Who are you talking about?"

She lowered her voice, as though it would be barbaric to invoke the name in anything less reverent than a hush, and said: *"The Circa family."*

Now, a good tour guide is also a diplomat. A good tour

guide does not, however strong the provocation, allow himself so untempered a comment as, *Ma'am, my dog has more culture than you.* A good tour guide does not, no matter how much he may wish to, call out to his fellow guides in the same venue, *This one wants to know about the* Circa *family! How stupid are yours?*

No, a good tour guide does what I did: cock his head slightly, purse his lips as if considering the matter seriously, then say, "I think perhaps you have misattributed some things."

Mrs. Taylor merely batted her eyes at me, as clear a sign of intellectual dismissal as I have ever encountered. A moment later she and her husband were dutifully admiring a Madonna and Child that had been painted Circa 1350. It wasn't a very good one, but even so accomplished a family of artists must be allowed its black sheep.

My obtuseness over the Circa question seemed to have convinced Mrs. Taylor that I was even less able to understand her than she'd thought. She compensated by drawing out her words even more agonizingly. "*Daaarrr*io," she asked me later, "how come in *Iiii*taly there are so *maaaa*ny A*merrrrr*ican *ressss*taurants?"

I began to explain that in the past few years, several fast-food chains had opened in the larger city centers, although fewer than in other countries—but I was interrupted by her husband. "No, Dario," he said, "my wife isn't referring to McDonald's, but to all the pizzerias we've seen. You Italians really seem to go for our pizza."

After a moment of genuine surprise, I tried to explain the origin of pizza—that it wasn't "theirs" at all, but one of the most ancient Italian recipes. From the implacable expression on their faces, I realized I wasn't getting through to them in the least. I imagined them back at home in the United States, dining on a hot Margherita or aromatic Neapolitan pizza, recalling between bites the nervy Italian guide who had tried to cheat them of their culinary heritage.

In fact, it wasn't only on the nationality of pizza that the Taylors had no doubts. They had certain granite certainties about the world that nothing could shake, not even solid evidence of the truth. Surely no one with even a shred of self-doubt could have gone into public looking the way Mrs. Taylor did. Nor walked beside her with pride, as her husband did. It was a kind of shared psychosis, certainly, but—like anything shared—it functioned paradoxically as a strength.

That evening I left them at their hotel. Although I had spoken English all day, and had taken particular care to speak it more gracefully than usual, Mrs. Taylor slllllooowly said goodbye to me, moving her lips as though she were speaking to someone deaf. She placed her right hand on her chest, then removed it and traced a circle between us with her index finger, from which I understood that she meant one day to return.

While she went up to her room, Mr. Taylor stayed behind to ask a few additional questions of me. He explained that they'd originally wanted to visit an art city called Florence, but because they couldn't find it on even the most detailed maps, they had come to Siena instead. From here they would continue to Firenze. "We've heard good things about it," he said, "and we thought it might be a valid alternative to Florence. What do you think?"

I considered explaining that a city couldn't be a "valid alternative" to itself, and that he had in fact made a rather common mistake. But looking at his suntanned face, into those eyes impervious to reason or enlightenment, I knew that he wouldn't thank me for it—would very likely not even believe me. What he really wanted was that I give him permission to do what he fully intended to do anyway. So I told him that Florence was indeed difficult to find and didn't offer any particularly exciting sights, while their next stop, Firenze, was surely a much better choice.

He thanked me, in the manner of someone thanking a garage mechanic for giving his Lamborghini a clean bill of health, and went off to join his wife.

A few years passed. One afternoon, while I was planting some rosemary in the garden, my cell phone rang. A bit annoyed, I pulled the hateful but useful contraption from my pocket with my dirt-encrusted hand.

From the other end a woman speaking poor Italian introduced herself by saying that she was calling on behalf of the Taylors, whom I had taken on a tour of Chianti some years before. Could I reserve a similar tour for a few friends of theirs?

In the background I could hear Mrs. Taylor directing the interpreter, ordering her to ask me many complicated questions. The poor woman was having trouble turning these queries into Italian, so I began replying in English, and she happily adapted to this initiative. The conversation became surreal: Mrs. Taylor posed the questions to her friend in English; the friend repeated them to me in English; I answered in English; and she conveyed my responses to Mrs. Taylor in English. Finally the woman asked her friend, "Excuse me, but why don't you just speak to Dario directly?"

I could hear my former client's reply: "Don't be ridiculous— he wouldn't understand me. He's *Italian.*"

LOVE AMONG THE RUINS

After the day I spent with Fosco, my search for old houses became so much an obsession that eventually I infected a group of friends with the same urge. There wasn't a weekend we didn't spend roaming the countryside on our scooters, looking for abandoned homesteads. These proved to be the perfect hideaways for rebellious, nonconformist teens. Here we could smoke joints, play the guitar, improvise feasts, and relish the unforgettable first fumblings of puppy love. For most of us the houses represented a sanctuary from the adult world and an authority we did not accept, but for me the interest went much farther. I wanted to know everything about the places and therefore began researching Chianti and its history. I learned that many houses had been built for military purposes and were destroyed and rebuilt a number of times before the fall of Siena to Florence in 1555. After that date these defensive outposts were turned over to private owners, who renovated them according to their needs.

The houses were constructed with local materials. Stones were removed from the fields during cultivation and set aside for use during winter, when farmers would add room after room to the main structure to accommodate the growth of their families.

The incredibly thick walls were built of dry stone, with no mortar, and the foundations weren't very deep. Yet hundreds of years have passed and they remain intact, testaments to the tremendous ability of those who built them. Many were constructed on hilltops—originally for strategic reasons, because they served as military fortifications, and later to take advantage of the drier wind, which helped ward off malaria, cold, and humidity.

The typical colonial house comprises a central tower around which additions sprang up in subsequent times, often built at different levels in a rather chaotic manner. The barnhouse was adjacent to the main structure, although the pigpen was detached from the main building to prevent the infiltration of the insufferable odor. Underground lay the wine cellar, on the ground floor the stables, and on the second floor a gigantic kitchen with a huge fireplace that was often the only source of heat. Often corridors didn't exist; to reach your bedroom, you had to pass through others', creating obvious impediments to privacy. Bathrooms did not exist at all, and it is not until the 1930s that we see the first additions of external walls creating an unpaved, unhygienic room with a hole in the ground (as in Fosco's house). Very rarely did the houses have a third story, though many had a little room in the tower used as a dovecote or to store the wooden barrels filled with precious *vin santo*.

Every time I discovered a new abandoned house, I called my group of friends, and even if it was for just a few hours, we restored life to the ruins. We lit a fire in the old hearth, roasted sausages, drank wine, and sang until the wee hours. Some of us, the boldest, even stayed the night.

When my brother, three years my senior, finally got his driver's license, we started roving around in his car, a black *deux chevaux* that he himself had restored and decorated with a beautiful painting on the hood. It was during one of these raids that we found a wonderful house in the middle of an oak forest. A typical colonial house, at first glance it appeared to be abandoned, if fairly recently. It wasn't in as bad a condition as most others. The windows were intact and the shutters closed; the entrance was tidy, the lawn well manicured and recently mowed. The front door swung open with just a little pressure, and we weren't assailed by the usual stuffy, humid smell typical of a house that had been closed for a long while. The place was completely furnished, the beds were made, and in the kitchen all was in order: The refrigerator was switched off and empty, the cutlery very neatly placed in the drawers, and in the pantry there was an ample supply of canned food.

We were very excited by our discovery and decided to return with some girlfriends.

Months passed during which it became a habit to pass entire days in "our" place. At long last we had a real house with true rooms and true beds, and even if these were ice cold, it was still, for us, a great conquest. And by then we had learned how to warm ourselves up!

Each time we returned the door had been magically repaired, and we, without thinking too much about this, forced it open again, allowing us access to this little corner of paradise that we fully considered our own. No one ever turned up beyond the door-repairing ghost. Still, we took the precaution of always leaving the car hidden in the forest a few hundred yards away, and making our way to the house on foot.

Eventually we began inviting friends and organizing dinners with hot meals cooked on the fireplace, followed by music, dancing, and joint smoking. Then one night, while we were sleeping it all off, there was a knock at the front door. Jolted awake, we looked at each other with terrified expressions, not having a clue what to do or daring to speak to each other for fear of being heard.

Then I had an epiphany: If the new arrival was knocking, he wasn't likely to be the owner of the house, or he'd simply have used his keys. Summoning my courage, I got up to go and greet him. My friends gestured their disapproval as I made my way to the entrance. Ignoring them, I arrived at the door and, completely naked, flung it open.

On the porch stood a middle-aged man who, with a rather astonished expression, kindly asked me, "Is Sara home?" I answered very firmly, as though I were the rightful owner of the house, "No, I'm sorry, Sara is out; she will return by nine." He took a furtive peek over my shoulders, then said good-bye and left.

When I closed the front door, I was in a cold sweat, my heart beating in my ears, but I felt exceptionally smart and cool: I had played the part so perfectly that the guy hadn't suspected a thing! As I slipped back under the covers, I actually thought we were rather lucky, because now we knew the name of one of the owners, and who could say but that one day this information would prove useful?

The man, of course, hadn't been fooled at all, and had immediately reported us to the local *carabinieri*. Fortunately they were slow in arriving. By then we'd already awakened and cleaned up, and were thus able to leave without a trace by jumping out the back window into the forest. But it had been too close a call.

Ten years passed—ten years during which I never again ventured anywhere near the place. Then, at a party, I met a

Swiss couple who were speaking fondly of their summer house. Their descriptions sounded oddly familiar to me. As soon as I realized that the house they were talking about was our old juvenile shelter, I asked the woman if her name was Sara. Surprised, she said yes.

I asked them innumerable questions about the house, and perhaps because of this interest, they invited me to dinner the following evening. Returning to the house had a strange effect on me, so much so that after a few glasses of wine I was dying to tell them of my experiences within these very walls. Some stronger instinct prevented me from doing so—perhaps fear of their reaction, or the simple respect I owed them for their invitation. In the end I kept my secret. But I remained untroubled by too much guilt for my adventures in the house. The sausages, the wine, and the girls were brought from outside, so that apart from the bedsheets we never touched anything that wasn't ours.

Today I am astonished to recall how innocently and naturally we did these things, but at the time we felt that all Chianti was a bit ours. Indeed, it was this sense of proprietorship that kept us from anything as malicious as vandalism.

■■

After I wore out my Vespa, I graduated to a more fashionable scramble bike, the legendary Cagiva Elephant 125, purchased after months of hard work at the Cecchi wine cellars. I ventured farther and farther down increasingly worse paths thanks to this agile cross-country vehicle. I sported a ridiculous dyed-blond Beatles hairstyle, wore the strangest hats imaginable, and was one of the first of my circle to have an ear pierced—a little silver ring dangled from my left lobe, provoking much gossip among the scandalized inhabitants of my village.

It was autumn, the most pleasant season of the year in

Chianti, the time of roasted chestnuts and porcini mushrooms. The daylight shortens and you begin huddling before the fireplace, sipping red wine and readying yourself for the imminent approach of winter. This is also the time that the grape reigns supreme: The harvest comes in, and the air is impregnated by the sweet aroma of the fruit, soon transformed to the sour scent of must when the yield is pressed in the tubs. Farmers' hands are stained purple, and their lips preserve the sweet flavor of the grapes "stolen" during the handpicking.

Under a dazzling and unusually warm sun, I was riding my bike along the dirt roads, taking in the beauties of the grape harvest. I noticed a path I had never seen before, a narrow pebble lane that penetrated a small wood of chestnut trees and ferns. Despite my bike being specially made for rough surfaces, I had no small difficulty staying upright on those slippery pebbles, and the vegetation thickened as I went till it became a dense and nearly impenetrable forest. By now I had learned that these old roads always led someplace, so I left the bike and continued on foot.

Suddenly an enormous wild boar sprang out of the bushes. I froze, and the terrifying beast assessed me carefully—then continued on its way. It was some minutes before I gained the courage to continue.

A bit farther on, the vegetation thinned, and then all at once I found myself in a open field upon which an abandoned house sat triumphantly. It was a splendid example of the archetype I had come to love—chicken court, pigpen, barn, stables under the main building, covered arched entrance, turret. This time I found the door hanging open, giving me reason to believe I was committing no violation.

I entered and found myself in a beautiful hall with an enormous fireplace still surrounded by old wooden benches. Unlike many other houses I'd seen, the roof, walls, and pavement were still intact, perhaps because the house had been abandoned in more recent times. In truth it wasn't completely deserted; one room housed a whole colony of bats, another a barn owl, while in the stables lived the biggest hornet hives I had ever seen.

I immediately fell in love with this new discovery, which I renamed simply *la casa*. I enlisted my friends to help clean it up, after which it became our new meeting place. The fireplace worked perfectly, so we brought in a grill and had many memorable barbecues.

Only about ten of us shared the secret of *la casa*, and for months this worked out beautifully. Then, close to New Year's Eve, someone had the idea to organize a big feast and to invite even more friends. I was very jealous of *la casa* and preferred not to share it with anyone else. The majority had voted in favor of the party, however, so I consented.

We put in a tremendous effort, polishing and cleaning everything. To render the place more festive, we bought decorations, candles, food, and wine in abundance.

In the end hundreds of uninvited people turned up along with the invited guests—so many new faces, friends of friends, people I had never seen before, that in no time the feast degenerated into a drunken brawl. When I saw the first flying bottles, I left in disgust.

On New Year's Day I returned to assess the damage. The fireplace had been destroyed, a dividing wall had been nearly pulled down, the walls were marred by obscene graffiti, and the pavement was completely obscured by the hundreds of broken bottles dashed atop it.

Hot, angry tears rolled down my cheeks. Surveying the

destruction, I felt as if I had betrayed *la casa*. The damage was too great for my friends and me to repair, and in any case the place was no longer a secret. I left, promising myself never to return.

But I did return, last year, out of curiosity and nostalgia. *La casa* was still abandoned, and I was astounded to discover that it still bore signs of that barbaric New Year's Eve of 1984.

MAY AND THE COLLECTOR

The Chianti countryside is now at its maximum splendor. The chestnuts and oaks are choked with leaves, and sweet fragrances scatter in the air. There is the scent of wisteria, the quintessence of the Tuscan spring; the potent aroma of honeysuckle, which wafts enormous distances; the balm of wild roses, lavender, and Spanish broom, and of the acacia that spills over the edges of the road with its abundance of delicate white flowers.

But above all, this is the month of the iris, pale blue and intensely aromatic. It grows wild but is often cultivated, and in May it is in full, resplendent flower. Entire fields of irises delight the eye. Farmers collect them and dry them in the sun, like bones; the warmer the sun, the stronger the fragrance. They will be sent to Florence and then to France, to be used for decoration or for perfume. In the past they were even used to flavor wines.

Wild thyme is now in flower as well, and treading on it releases its heady scent; likewise marjoram, fennel, catmint, rosemary, and sage. May is the month the nightingales sing day into dusk, and in the evening fireflies reappear.

May is also the month I first met John Aiello, some eight years ago. I went to fetch him in Florence on a glorious morning, the first of the year on which it was clement enough to drive with the sunroof open. The warm sun had put me in a good mood, and despite the usual Florentine chaos, I was singing at the top of my lungs, ignoring the traffic and the chorus of car horns surrounding me. I found John waiting in front of a modest hotel in the city center, accompanied by his brother and sister-in-law.

The tour went without a hitch; the four of us passed a perfectly splendid day roaming the sweet hills of Chianti. When we returned to the hotel in the evening, John asked me if I would accompany him to the station where he was to catch a train for Milan, and without thinking twice I consented. He dashed up to his room. When he returned I noticed with surprise that apart from the customary baggage, he also had a small antique table. "And this?" I asked, pointing to it.

He shot me an exultant look and said, "I bought it yesterday from a dealer here in Florence! I think it'll look great in the entrance to my house." Noting his apparent passion for old furniture, I told him that if he was interested in buying similar objects I could take him to the largest antiques market in Italy, in the Tuscan city of Arezzo. He seemed very excited by my offer and vowed to return as soon as possible to take me up on it.

Watching him enter the station, precariously balancing the fragile table atop his luggage, I couldn't imagine how it would survive both the train and the even-more-restricted jet to the States. But somehow John managed it. I later learned that the beloved piece is proudly sitting in his entrance hall.

John has some curious Italian origins. Unlike most Italo-Americans, whose families emigrated from the south, John's antecedents are only half southern; the other half hail from the extreme north, from a small town on the Austrian border. A third-generation American—his grandparents landed in Philadelphia in the 1930s—John, like many Italians, was reared to forget most of his ethnic traditions and origins. He's an American through and through—what we call a "DOCG American" (after the label of authenticity on our wine bottles)—and doesn't speak even a word of Italian. But this doesn't prevent him from coming twice a year for brief visits to the country of his ancestors.

Considered the family genius—he's a successful attorney who runs a prestigious law firm in Washington, D.C., as well as a gifted pianist—John is resolutely single. He has never been married, although I have seen him in very attractive company. Lean and not very tall, he dresses in a casual but studied way that confers on him a kind of 1960s-intellectual appearance. Thick glasses and a rather distinctive mustache bring to mind Groucho Marx, whom he resembles in his eccentric wit as well.

The year after our first encounter, he returned as promised, and I took him to the Arezzo market, which is held on the first weekend of every month in the city of Piero della Francesca (or, if you prefer, of the movie *Life Is Beautiful*). The market is an important event in which vendors from every part of Italy participate, and where among the heaps of cheap rubbish it's possible to find an occasional piece of real quality. There are objects to satisfy all types of collectors—phone cards, stamps, coins, postcards, old clothes, and the "new" antiques of the 1970s, as well as the genuine articles.

I noticed immediately that John had a good eye for spotting fakes, and soon I became equally aware of his highly distinctive taste. I expected him to be attracted to the traditional Tuscan peasant-style furniture so popular now in Italy, but instead he pursued the seventeenth-century Genovese *Risorgimento* style, with particular interest in the imitations made at the turn of last century. As soon as he saw a piece of furniture made out of dark wood with carved curls, or figures of angels and devils, he stopped and excitedly asked me to glean as much information as possible. If a piece lacked any such opulent characteristics, he ignored it.

That first day, I became the interpreter for many seemingly endless negotiations. Eventually he purchased a marble table with an inlaid wooden base, ornamented with a complicated flower pattern, and a very dark oaken wardrobe with heavy, somewhat bizarre carvings. After having arranged the shipment with the dealer and sorting out all the documents, we went to celebrate with some gigantic steaks and a bottle of robust red wine; a good purchase always must be "wet" for good luck, he said.

On the road back we were relaxed and happy. The day had been pleasant, the visit to the market had borne fruit, and all had been for the best—until at a certain point I noticed that the car was pulling away from me. "John," I said, "we may have a problem . . ." A moment later I heard the telltale *flap-flap-flap*. I parked on the side of the road and changed the punctured tire, obtaining some terrible, greasy stains on my white shirt. Then we set off again.

I left the car in a no-parking area close to the hotel for *just* the amount of time necessary to accompany John into the hotel—then returned to find a brilliant pink ticket waving at me from the windshield. For a moment I thought there might be a reason the evening had started to turn, but soon the two minor incidents passed from my mind.

The next year John returned again and requested an oenogastronomic tour of the Langhe in the Piedmont area in northwest Italy, after which he wanted to return to Tuscany and of course go the "usual" market in Arezzo. I went to pick him up at the Milan airport but had to cool my heels for a few hours because his plane was delayed. When he finally arrived we left immediately for Alba, a town famous for its white truffles.

The first thing I asked him was whether he'd received the furniture he'd purchased on his previous trip. Laughing, he replied, "Oh, sure, I got it all right! But the marble table was cracked into about a thousand pieces." I was furious with myself; I'd had a hunch not to trust that antiquarian. I promised John that in the future I would personally supervise the packing and choose a reputable courier.

After two days of big meals in the best restaurants of the area, downed with equally excellent bottles of Barolo, Barbera, Barbaresco, and Grignolino, we started our six-hour sojourn to Tuscany. On our way down from Piedmont, on the highway near Bologna, one of my front wheels flew off and we started zigzagging perilously. My life flashed before my eyes, accompanied by a soundtrack of John's startled shouts. Fortunately I managed to keep the car on the road until I could steer it, with no small difficulty, into the emergency lane. For three hours we awaited the arrival of the tow truck; then, given the impossibility of repairing the car anytime soon, we continued to Siena by taxi.

The following day my mechanic lent me a car and went personally to Sasso Marconi to repair mine. In the meantime John and I were still somewhat shocked by the whole incident; to calm ourselves, we went for a tour of Pienza and Montalcino, where we drank some stunning vintage Brunellos. We stayed out very late, drinking and chatting, and when we returned I decided to drive John directly to his hotel in the historic center of Siena. This is a pedestrian area totally closed to traffic, but I was convinced that at that time of night there was little risk of meeting any traffic wardens.

Alas, there they were, at two in the morning, as if they had been lying in wait for me. I was ticketed and fined. And of course my mood was soured.

Next day, at the Arezzo market, John bought two bedside tables and a console from which two terrible carved lions emerged, ready to devour anyone who ventured too near. At the end of the day, I took him to the local station so he could board a train to Milan, where he had booked a flight home. But there was something wrong at the station; it was still and silent, with none of the usual roar of engines or shriek of whistles.

We had arrived in the midst of a six-hour strike. John was in danger of missing his flight home. Feeling somewhat responsible, I offered to take him to Milan myself. After five hours of breakneck driving, we arrived at Malpensa Airport just in time. Our sense of triumph evaporated, however, when we learned that the flight had been canceled due to heavy fog.

Exhausted and upset, we headed back to the car, having before us the depressing prospect of trying to find a place to spend the night. As John opened the passenger door, he put a foot deep into some dog droppings. We laughed wildly, hoping that this crowning ignominy would signal a turnaround in our luck.

It didn't. We spent four hours in fruitless search of a hotel room; thanks to a conference in town, there wasn't a vacancy to be had. We were forced to sleep in the car. We awakened the next morning with aches and pains in places we didn't know we had. The fog had gone, but I was shocked to find another ticket on the windshield. Too late, I saw that I had parked in a space reserved for the handicapped.

Throughout all these nerve-shredding experiences, John managed to keep things light by regaling me with stories of the more bizarre cases he'd handled in court. My favorite remains that of the two inner-city couples who were copulating simultaneously in the same car—one couple in the front seat, the other in back. At a certain point the man in front asked his friend in the back if he had an extra condom. The backseat man said, "No, but if you wait a minute, you can have mine." The astonishing result of this generosity was that the woman in the front seat became pregnant by the man in the back—and sued both men for the outrage.

Each time John told a story of this kind, he doubled up with laughter so that his head nearly banged against his knees, and with his fist he beat his thigh repeatedly. Once after having shared an anecdote of this nature (it might have been the same one), he laughed for five uninterrupted minutes and then for some time afterward intermittently repeated the punch line and giggled to himself.

Another year passed, and John returned—this time with his girlfriend. I met them at the airport, but on our drive to Tuscany, we were stalled in traffic for four hours due to a terrible accident between two trucks. John tried to lighten the tension by telling jokes, but his girlfriend was bored stiff and kept stifling yawns. She also suffered badly from carsickness. When traffic finally did begin moving again, we had to leave the highway several times in search of the pills that were her only remedy—and that unfortunately seemed to be stocked by no pharmacy in all of Italy.

She also had what I considered a far greater disorder. John and I dragged her to all the best restaurants of Tuscany to introduce her to new flavors and textures, but she exclusively ordered tuna fish. Tuna and a green salad, tuna sandwiches, tuna spreads, tuna you-name-it. This worried me to the extent that, during a visit to an important church, when her attention was distracted, I took John aside and whispered, "My friend, never trust a woman who eats only tuna fish!" My advice was meant seriously; I am, after all, an Italian. But he exploded into laughter that resounded deafeningly through the church and beat his fist merrily on my shoulder. When he had calmed down, he quietly reassured me, "Don't worry, buddy, I have no intention of marrying her!"

We then returned to the car—or, rather, where we'd left the car. An old man seated on a bench, puffing calmly on a Tuscan cigar, told us that he'd seen it being towed away by the traffic wardens. I couldn't understand why; it seemed to me that I'd parked perfectly legally. After a few hours I managed to track it down, and once we'd paid the heavy fine to recover it, John and I began seriously to wonder whether his visits provoked some sort of hostility from the cosmos. His girlfriend just stared at me nastily.

The following day we made our way to Arezzo, driving through a disastrous hailstorm that destroyed many crops. At the market John fell in love with a ridiculously large coatrack, but wasn't certain it would fit in his house. In the end he said "what the heck" and bought it anyway—along with a pink glass chandelier. After yet another train strike, plus major problems at the customs desk (he had close to fifteen bottles of wine in his suitcase), he and his girlfriend were finally able to board their flight back home.

A few months later he phoned to alert me that he wanted to buy a bed and thus needed to return to Arezzo. I took advantage of the call to satisfy my curiosity about the coatrack. "Did you manage to fit it in the house?"

"No," he said, "but I found a way around the problem." "How?" I asked. "Easy—I bought a bigger house." While he was laughing, I could actually hear him beating his leg.

This time John was accompanied by another woman, about whom he seemed very enthusiastic. "You'll like this one," he assured me. "She isn't a spoiled wet blanket like the last one." Thinking ruefully of that earlier romance, he shook his head and said, "You know, she kept insisting I buy a Cadillac—she didn't think someone in my position should be driving around in an Oldsmobile!"

The new girlfriend was dressed head to toe in black leather, with high boots that ventured up over the knee. She had a splendid head of fiery red hair, and true to the stereotype she was definitely an explosive sort. This was her first time away from the States, and she had myriad difficulties adapting to Italy. She was unable to figure out how to flush the toilets (which function is often, in Italy, accomplished by a foot pedal or with photoelectric cells) and could never manage to find the light switches. Once she stormed out of the women's room in a restaurant shrieking, "Does anything in this goddamn country *work*?"

This time John was lucky: He found not only his bed but also a love seat in the "Aiello style," as it had by now been termed by the warehouseman I used for his shipments. During a long negotiation with a stubborn dealer, John's new girlfriend asked where she could find a pharmacy. I explained that, this being Sunday, only one would be open to serve the town, and that it was likely to be a bit out of our way; we would need to leave the market and go by car. I asked if her need was urgent, because once we'd left the market we wouldn't be readmitted.

"*Very* urgent," she insisted.

We finally found the pharmacy. After a few minutes inside, she returned with a little box of dental floss. I felt like strangling her.

Fortunately John's next visit to Italy was a return to the basics—just the two of us. This time, after the obligatory visit to the market—where he bought more Aiello-style furniture and a couple of kitschy marble lions—we spent some time touring Perugia and Assisi. When we said good-bye, we suddenly realized, with some alarm, that the weather had been good, the trains had been on time, there had been no strikes, no accidents, no tickets, no traffic, no tow trucks, no difficult girlfriends—everything had gone absolutely perfectly. Two days later Assisi was virtually leveled by an earthquake.

John's visits are by now part of my annual routine; the year just wouldn't seem complete without our trip to the Arezzo market. The last time we spoke, he described his new house, full of white Italian marble. The attachment he feels to Italy is tremendous: Even as a third-generation American who can't speak the language, he feels a compulsion to come here at least once a year to "recharge." If he doesn't have much time for travel, he'll come just for a weekend. He unabashedly adores everything Italian: the Parmesan cheese (so much so that I once took him to Parma to see it being made), the fine Tuscan olive oil, the Piedmontese wines, and all the unique Mediterranean flavors. I couldn't say to which of his Italian origins his character owes the most: the ambitious north, or the sensual south. Both are strong in him.

Many times he has invited me to his home in Washington, D.C. I've yet to go, but having seen many of the spooky, almost Gothic pieces with which he's furnished it, I have always imagined his house to look something like that of the Addams Family.

By the way, while writing this chapter, I received a phone call from John. Of his last shipment, half arrived smashed, the other half not at all. The Aiello effect strikes again!

INTERVALLO

The Dutch

While Americans form the majority of my tours, I've had the privilege of escorting people from all over the world—so many, in fact, that to mention them all would require hundreds of additional pages; I'd rather just save them for a sequel. But in the interest of fair play, I'll take this moment to give my American friends a breather and turn instead to a group from a very different place indeed.

■■

The Dutch is the name I use to define a happy bunch who hail from Holland, whom I have had the pleasure of squiring around Tuscany several times. Over the years these customers have become good friends—so much so that the very term *customers* seems a bit formal for them. Each time they visit Italy, they book my services for at least a week. The group comprises three couples:

Sjaak and Hanneke. Sjaak is the leader of the pack, the first to voice an opinion and the one who gets the final word. Of typically open Flemish features, he wears a perpetually happy expression spiced by a bit of devil in the eyes, so that he seems always to be taking the piss out of you. No matter the weather, Sjaak wears a vest full of pockets in which he stores an exhaustive range of tools and gadgets—pocket screwdrivers, flashlights, small knives, you name it. Sjaak is also the cashier for the group, and his place in the van is up front, next to me.

As is true of all successful leaders, Sjaak is partnered by an equally remarkable spouse. Reserved, kindly, and highly refined, Hanneke seems always to have even the most difficult situation under control, and gives the impression that she is the one who wears the pants. With but a gesture or a quick glance, she can alter Sjaak's behavior instantly. Inseparable, they own and manage a business together. With six visits in six consecutive years, they are, I think, the soul of the group.

Han and Jeanne are the next most frequent visitors, with five visits under their belts. Co-workers in the computer field, they're both of robust constitution and are connoisseurs of delicate wines and foods. Han, who completed an advanced sommelier course, is the group's authority on wine, differing from the usual expert only in that he never spits out what he tastes. Equally remarkable is his passion for steak *fiorentina*. Jeanne loves wine as well, but unlike Han never says no to beer or hard liquor; she has been known to concoct some interesting mixtures, even in the morning. Though not particularly loquacious, both are very pleasant company.

Renè and Bianca complete the group, although to date they have visited Chianti only twice. It's probably due to his goodhearted character, but Renè is mercilessly teased by the others. With his unflappable, childlike demeanor, he gives the impression that nothing is sufficient to anger him, and even Bianca seems to treat him more like a son than a husband. Like the other couples, Renè and Bianca work together, managing a restaurant. My first contact with the group was through an agri-tourist agency; the owner asked me if I would accompany four Dutch visitors for some day trips, specifying that they had declared themselves particularly interested in tasting local wines and foods. This was at the beginning of my career as a guide, and I had always organized trips for one or two days tops, so it was a daunting prospect to be in charge of these clients for an entire week. In addition, I knew nothing of the habits and pref-erences of the Dutch, having thus far only worked with British and American customers. To guard against making any mis-takes, I drew up a rather elastic program that could be changed to suit their requirements.

When I arrived for the first time at the agritourist center, a small, out-of-the-way farm in the Chianti hills, I was surprised to find that these Dutch had not rented any kind of vehicle despite the fact that the place, admittedly fascinating in itself, wasn't reachable by any other means. I talked through the pro-gram I'd customized for them: Chianti the first day, Crete the second, Montalcino the third, and so on, a region a day, until the sixth day, when I proposed to take them shopping in Florence. They looked at me with wide eyes, as though just the recitation of the agenda had worn them out. "No, no," Sjaak protested, "we're here to relax, so let's just take it nice and easy. And please, no cities or shopping—we have enough of that in Holland."

And so the next morning I took them on my standard, leisurely Chianti tour, with a visit to the winery, the Etruscan tomb, the smaller vineyard, a stop at a local village, and then lunch.

After a *crostino* appetizer, beautifully cooked by Gina and Carla, they asked me to make the courses arrive more slowly, because they absolutely weren't in a hurry and had no real urge to get up from the table anytime soon. I began to wonder: Were they truly interested in the archaeology and history of Chianti? Or were the gastronomy and oenology of the area more what they were seeking? . . . The enormous amounts of food they tucked away soon removed any doubt. These Dutch ate and drank like no one I'd ever seen before.

After lunch, basking in the contentment of a good meal and good wine, we got to know each other a bit better. So I was only slightly surprised when they asked me to stop at a bar along the way. Here they consumed enough grappa to stagger a whole company of *Alpini* militiamen—and never showed the slightest sign of drunkenness. Amazed, I took them back to the hotel, thinking that they must now surely collapse in their rooms, their heroic bout of drinking taking a delayed toll on them.

The next day, as soon as I parked in the hotel courtyard, the manager came out to greet me, waving his arms. "Dario," he gasped in astonishment, "yesterday your Dutch drained my wine cellar dry! I've never seen anything like it!" I now wondered if I would even see them this morning; if I did, surely they would be shambling, depleted husks, each with a gray complexion and killer hangover.

Instead they showed up right on time, looking fresh as daisies, obviously rested and in bright good humor. "Dario," they asked all at once, "where are we going to eat today?"

From that moment on, I knew exactly how to accommodate them: All I had to do each day was take them on some brief morning activity, find a bar where we could down a few beers while waiting for the lunch hour, and then whisk them off to one of the best restaurants in the area. With the Dutch it was perfectly normal to be the first customers seated and the last ones to depart. Lunch typically lasted a leisurely five hours.

They were never other than merry at table, all eating and jabbering and laughing at the same time. They would try anything without bothering to look at the cost; it wasn't unusual for their lunch bill to exceed a million *lire*. They could empty up to fourteen wine bottles without appearing even slightly tipsy. Those lunches were, for me, a great boon, because I had the opportunity to taste many rare and expensive wines that I could otherwise afford only occasionally, if at all. So I let myself go and ate and drank like a pig.

It rained hard for the remainder of the week, and I had the impression that they were increasingly less interested in agritourism; for that reason I thought, when their trip was over, that they would not return. But in 1995 they contacted me again, asking whether I could find them affordable lodgings in a central location, and also if I would rent a larger van to carry them—this time they would be six.

They arrived in early October with Renè and Bianca. I collected them at the small airport in Florence, took them from the chaos of the city and down the winding, bendy *chiantigiana* road into Tuscany. Knowing how to please them, I stopped at the first available bar, where, with the excuse that they had to wet their throats after the dry air on the plane, they drank an incredible amount of Prosecco and beer.

For lunch we stopped at Fosco's place. He sat us under the shade of a large oak and served us a sumptuous meal composed of Tuscan appetizers, tagliatelle in wild boar sauce, *ribollita*, an abundant tray of mixed, grilled meats, gigantic *fiorentina* steaks, and stewed rabbit with olives—all of which the group washed down with the most expensive vintage Brunellos. Afterward, when they complained of needing some sugar, Fosco brought out a tasting of each of his best sweets (cooked cream, *tiramisù*, homemade jam tarts) and some different types of *vin santo* and sweet sparkling wine.

We had no sooner gotten on the road than we found ourselves stopping at the bar in Vagliagli where, "for digestive purposes," we had a tasting of various grappas and *amari*.

By the time we finished, it was almost time for dinner, so we moved from the bar to the adjacent restaurant and started again from the beginning—porcini mushroom appetizers, polenta served in hare sauce, and crepes stuffed with white truffles, followed by casseroled guinea fowl, wild boar, and still more desserts—everything accompanied by bottles of Chianti Classico, Nobile di Montepulciano, and fortified wines for dessert. Toward midnight, unsteady on my feet, I accompanied the happy group back to the hotel, where Han proposed some grappa "nightcaps." I fled in terror.

When I arrived to pick them up the next morning, I found them again in peak condition, relaxing in the bar with some enormous beers.

The first question, as usual, was, "Dario, where are we going to eat today?"

"Montalcino," I replied, still a bit abashed by their one-track minds.

"Ah! The town of the Brunello wine and the *pici* with truffles," they added, licking their lips.

And off we went. Before arriving at Montalcino we made two stops for beer. In town I proposed a short walk, but as soon as we reached the main square, they said that they couldn't return to Holland without passing an hour or two at an old-style Tuscan coffee bar; so once again we found ourselves drining absolute rivers of Prosecco. After having drained the ninth bottle, to the stupefaction of our waiter, who had clearly never seen anything like it in his life, we got up to go and eat in the adjoining restaurant. Although it was his day off, Mario had remained open as a favor to me. What's more, seeing that the weather was splendid, he'd set the table outside, at the most advantageous point in the garden, from which we enjoyed a splendid view of Crete and the Val d'Orcia. Mario came to greet us himself, holding a wicker basket filled with porcini and ovolo mushrooms, and with a wink told us that in just a few moments a friend of his would arrive with some truffles he'd just unearthed. No sooner had he said this than the friend entered the garden with his truffle-sniffing dog close behind. Under our very noses he unrolled a white paper wrapping to reveal a bounty of the precious tubers. As soon as they were freed from their confinement, they released their uncanny aroma, making our mouths water.

Mario put them to good use for us, whipping up a series of black and white truffle sauces on homemade sliced bread, followed by a raw mushroom salad, taglierini with truffles, tagliatelle with porcini, steak *fiorentina* for Han, gigantic grilled porcini heads, and, for dessert, various seasoned pecorino cheeses and homemade honey ice cream. At close to five in the afternoon, when with tremendous difficulty we managed to stand, I counted twelve empty bottles of Brunello, two of Moscadello, and one of grappa.

We took a more direct road back, but only reached Siena after two more beer stops. In the narrow alley that led to the hotel, I scraped the rental van against the wall, badly scratching the whole flank of the vehicle, to roars of Dutch laughter. For days afterward they teased me continually about this incident.

That evening the group decided to dine in the hotel.

Gratefully, I left them, and as soon as I got home I made myself a cup of hot tea and went straight to bed.

The following morning, while I waited for them in the reception area, the hotel director came to me and said, "Don't you feed those Dutch people when you take them out? Last night they asked me just to fix them a snack, and by the time I was finished with them, I'd used up everything in the kitchen!" Then, with a half-amused expression, he added, "Please also do me the favor of explaining to them that the bottles on the mantelpiece were intended for decoration, and that we made an exception for them only because of their insistence and apparent need." As he said this, he stood aside and gestured toward the empty shelves around the fireplace. I laughed and shrugged. What could I do? They were the Dutch!

Just then they arrived, punctual and merry as ever. "Montepulciano!" I exclaimed, not waiting for the inevitable question. "Ah," they exclaimed as we headed out to the van, "the land of the *vino nobile!*"

Again the usual routine: two short stops for beer and Prosecco, a quick look at the village, then off to the restaurant to begin a new day of stuffing ourselves, this time with venison and boar ham appetizers, barley soup, *pappa al pomodoro*, tripe, pork livers, stewed duck, and fresh desserts. As ever, there was much joy at the table, and even greater quantities of *nobile* wine. On the way back they sang Dutch folk songs very loudly and very long.

The following morning they had chosen to go all the way to the sea, to Porto Santo Stefano on the south Tuscan coast. No prizes for guessing the purpose of the trip—the area boasts a renowned seafood restaurant. This time we started with oysters and a warm octopus salad, followed by clams, squid, mussels, and shrimp in cocktail sauce with anchovies. Then came a tasting of *cacciucco* (a local fish soup), a delectable homemade pasta with crab sauce, and risotto cooked in cuttlefish ink. For the main course there was a tray of grilled lobster, shrimp, and a great sargo. To cleanse our palates after that triumph of fish, we were served the most delicate lemon sorbet.

It was a beautiful day, and Sjaak said, "Why don't we rent a boat and explore along the coast?" The idea was greeted enthusiastically, so we went to the little mall and found a fisherman who, as soon as he saw the hundreds of thousands of *lire* being waved in front of him, gladly consented to take us—although the sea was starting to get a little turbulent.

We left under a dazzling sun, but once we got out of the port, the going got tough. Every wave soaked us completely; by the time we returned, we were thoroughly drenched. The Dutch didn't care in the least. They continued laughing and joking, very happy to have had their unusual cruise along the spectacular coastline of Mont Argentario.

As we neared Siena, despite still being soaked, they asked if it was possible to stop for a pizza. Renè, who was the wettest of us all, had gotten completely undressed in the van, paying no heed to the others' teasing comments; now he entered the pizzeria wearing only his underwear. Paola, one of the owners of the place, pretended to be scandalized. She took a big white paper tablecloth, folded it into a triangle, wrapped one of the sides around his waist, tucked the tail between his legs, bound it all together on his other hip with a safety pin, and then said, "Now you can sit down." When he entered the dining room in that enormous diaper, there was a moment of silence—then virtually all the diners burst into laughter.

Despite their enormous lunch only a few hours earlier, my

friends ate two pizzas each and drank an incredible amount of beer. Renè play-acted the big baby, going from table to table and leaving the diners in stitches. After the pizzas were gone, they started tossing back an incredible amount of grappa, and for the first time the near-legendary Sjaak showed signs of inebriation. On his fifth glass he started raising the volume of his voice and making strange speeches, and after his ninth, overcome with enthusiasm, he said, "Dario, next year Hanneke and I will return to Siena for the Palio, and we will bring you luck!" Knowing that my *contrada* had not had a victory in decades, he leaned in close and whispered, *"The Caterpillar will finally win again!"*

"Consider yourselves booked!" I said.

That night poor Sjaak staggered back to the hotel with the aid of the others, but the following morning he was—what else?—rested and fit and more than ready to begin drinking and eating. In San Gimignano, ignoring the dazzling towers, we headed straight for a restaurant and, apart from the dozen or so bottles of wine and grappa, consumed a menu composed of Tuscan appetizers, risotto with asparagus tips, ravioli stuffed with wild herbs, pork cooked in fennel sauce, roasted potatoes, roast beef and spinach flan, and, for dessert, a Fedora cake.

On their last day I drove the group to Florence, and while awaiting their flight home, I helped them drink the bar dry.

The following year Sjaak and Hanneke kept their promise and returned specifically for the Palio. It was August 1996, and the Caterpillar earned a thrilling victory, bringing home a Palio for the first time in forty-one years.

THE BLACK ROOSTER

The 1980s passed into history, as did the glorious era of partying in abandoned houses. We were growing up, and increasingly adulthood dispersed our group; some of us began working, others moved to the city to attend the university, still others married. A few have since vanished completely from my life.

In addition, most of the old farmhouses were purchased and transformed into comfortable vacation homes. Suddenly all Chianti was awakening from the torpor of abandonment. At the same time, my job at the winery became less and less satisfying. I wanted to create my own job, and do it on my own terms—in other words, I wanted independence. But what could I do? The only marketable talents I had were my fluency in English and my thorough knowledge of the area. I started wondering whether it might be possible to join the two together, offering my services to tourists who wanted to see the real Chianti.

After having reflected a long time and assessing all the risks, and without any encouragement whatsoever (quite the opposite), I quit my job and threw myself enthusiastically into my new profession. My first task was to obtain the right permits, and after that to create a logo, in which I incorporated a black rooster, the symbol of Chianti.

To understand the iconic status of the black rooster, we must go back to the year 1206, when the perpetually warring Sienese and Florentines negotiated a peace treaty that was, as usual, to prove very short-lived. During the negotiations the representatives of the two republics could not agree on where to establish the border between their states. The Florentines wanted the line drawn farther south; the Sienese, obviously, farther north. To avoid useless quarreling they decided to settle the question with a contest. The best rider from each town would leave his city and travel the same road until the two met. At that exact point the new border would be established. Since there were no watches to synchronize, it was decided that the riders should begin when the cock crowed.

Having settled the rules, the two cities prepared for the competition by choosing their fastest horses and most accomplished riders. But while the Sienese respected the integrity of the game, the Florentines, as usual, found a way to cheat. The night before the contest, they didn't feed their rooster; then, during the night, they had someone parade close to the henhouse bearing a large candle. When the hungry bird saw the candlelight, he took it for the first rays of dawn and, eager to be fed, started crowing at the top of his lungs. Whereupon the Florentine rider hopped onto his horse and galloped away.

The Sienese representatives sent to guarantee Florentine compliance could not deny, when presented with this outrage, that the letter of the law had been followed, however its spirit may have been violated. Therefore the Florentine knight legitimately obtained a few hours' advantage over his poor Sienese counterpart, who had scarcely had time to leave his city before meeting his adversary on the road.

We have no evidence that this story is factual, and it well

may be apocryphal; but, curiously, the point at which the two would likely have met does correspond to an ancient borderline between the two cities. And although today the border lies equidistant between Siena and Florence, in the northern part of Chianti, which is closest to Florence, the people retain some vestiges of Florentine dialect and traditions, as if testifying to the truth of the legend.

(In all fairness I must admit that version of the story I've just told is Sienese. The Florentines repudiate it and insist that the whole contest was conducted fairly. But I persist in my belief in the Sienese version. After all, no *fiorentino* could beat a Sienese without cheating!)

In 1924 the producers of Chianti Classico wine, unified as a consortium, chose as their symbol a black rooster in memory of their honest ancestors. That same black rooster sits proudly on the neck of every bottle produced today, as an indication of the quality of the wine produced in our hills.

So the black rooster—symbol of Chianti, its history, and its wine—was a natural choice for my logo. But since I intended to operate in other areas of Tuscany as well, I added a cypress tree, which is the symbol of the entire region, appearing in virtually every painting, photograph, and souvenir postcard.

Once I'd designed the logo, the name followed naturally: Rooster Tours. I then chose an enticing photo of the Chianti hills, wrote some copy, printed up the whole thing on black coated paper, and, *ecco*, I had a promotional brochure.

Not wanting to overrun the area with hordes of tourists, I decided to limit my groups to a maximum of five. Then with my few savings I bought, secondhand, a four-wheel-drive mini van—a curious, egg-shaped vehicle particularly suited to traveling over bumpy, dusty roads. It seated five comfortably.

Next came the tough part: finding customers. Since I had no contacts with travel agencies in any foreign countries, I thought it would be a good idea to make my services known in area hotels.

I suspected that, given my youth and my bohemian look, no one would take me seriously in the more elegant hotels. So I cut my hair, removed my earrings, and purchased both an Armani suit and a briefcase for my brochures. And in this manner I set out to woo all the major hotels in Siena and Florence. I was very shy, and each time I introduced myself to a concierge, I blushed and began to stutter. Often I had the impression that the people I was talking to didn't have a clue what I was trying to offer. Some discouraged me, saying my plan would never work; others cut me off with, "If someone asks for such a service, we will contact you"; still others pretended to be enthusiastic but, as soon as my back was turned, balled up my expensive brochures and tossed them into a wastebasket.

Most of the concierges, however, seemed more interested in taking a percentage on the tours—something I wouldn't have denied them, if they only gave me a chance to speak! In total I visited more than 400 hotels, leaving in each reception area an entire stack of brochures.

Time passed, and no one called. This was before the cellular era, so I spent entire days at home with my eyes glued to the telephone. If I had to leave the house, immediately on returning I would leap on my answering machine, only to find it bereft of messages. In desperation I started stopping tourists on the road, handing them brochures. Seeing me with my crew cut and black suit and tie, most people hurried away from what appeared to be an attempt to convert them to Mormonism.

After this initial defeat I decided not to trust the hotel

receptionists to do my work for me. In order to learn whether there was any genuine interest in my services, I proceeded to Plan B, and employed the talents of the impressive, if wholly imaginary, Mr. Hobbs. After each visit to a hotel, I headed for the nearest phone booth. There I would dial the number of the hotel I had just left. "Good afternoon," I'd say in a thick cockney accent, "my name is Hobbs, and I'm calling from London. I want to reserve a room, and also want to know if you have any tours that take people around the Chianti area." Invariably the same person who five minutes before had shown me so much enthusiasm would say, "I'm sorry, sir, we have no such service."

Finally, after the twentieth such reply, I gave one of them a nudge: "You mean you don't know Chianti Rooster Tours?"

"No sir."

"But are you sure?" Mr. Hobbs persisted. "Chianti Rooster Tours by Dario Castagno? Surely you've got the brochure."

"No sir, I'm terribly sorry."

At that point I snapped. Becoming Dario Castagno again, I said in my roughest Tuscan, "Listen, you bastard, if you opened the drawer in front of you, you'd find enough Chianti Rooster brochures to #&*@*$%#!"—then slammed the phone down in a genuine fury.

The situation was starting to have repercussions. Apart from some imminent financial problems, I was slipping into what could be a deep depression. I simply couldn't understand why no one was calling me. Everywhere else in Chianti, tourism was booming. I felt like a failure; all my enthusiasm and expectations of success suddenly evaporated, leaving nothing in their place.

But true desperation would have led me back to the winery—and the idea of returning there, tail between my legs, to the intense satisfaction of all those who'd discouraged me from going out on my own, was unendurable.

I had to hold on, and have faith.

JUNE AND THE DISCONTENTED

Summer already, and the roses are at the apex of their splendor. The hills are painted yellow by the Spanish broom, which smothers the valleys with its heady scent. Wildflowers pop up even in the more rocky and sterile fields. Cornflowers, poppies, and chamomile pepper the meadows, as does the deep salmon-pink sainfoin. This used to be grown as a fodder crop, and you'll occasionally see entire fields of it.

Flocks of migratory birds stop in Chianti to take a night's rest; in the morning you may be awakened by the tremendous clamor they make while frenetically passing along travel information before resuming their flight north. The sweet, golden song of the oriole is frequently heard, but the singer itself is difficult to spot among the branches. The much less timid hoopoes, whose elegant plumage has served as inspiration to haute couture designers, consent to be admired while they peck for food at the hard bark of the trees.

At sunset the skies are aswarm with bats, and all night long the shrieks of owls curdle the blood.

One spring I agreed to a tour for two women who had contacted me through an elegant residence in Siena. One had come to Italy in order to choose hotels, restaurants, and other spots of interest for a June tour she was organizing for her husband and another couple. We visited some of the more expensive and elegant hotels of Chianti, and in every one this lady collected detailed information, carefully inspecting the rooms, suites, baths, lounges, restaurants, swimming pools, and any other features and amenities. Despite her near-maniacal fussiness, she relaxed when the day was over and became friendly and personable. She seemed satisfied with her research and apparently with me as well, because she booked me for two days when she and her party returned.

A month later she contacted me to confirm and to send the schedule she had prepared. I was very curious to see which hotel she had chosen and was astonished to find that her party would spend their three nights in Chianti in three different lodgings, moving every day from one hotel to the next over a total range of only about 30 miles. I thought this a highly awkward and inconvenient idea, but decided that the group must be as enthusiastic about luxury accommodations as their organizer was and wanted to experience as many as possible.

I went to pick them up on a warm June morning. I didn't find my original client awaiting me, although we had been in contact about arrangements up to the day before, but one of her friends was there. This woman was done up in a rather heavy wool suit, on which a series of shiny gold buttons protruded, complemented by gold-buckled high-heeled shoes.

Wow, I thought, *a perfect Mirjana Markovic style!* This was at the height of the NATO attempt to end the massacres in Yugoslavia, and images of Slobodan Milosevic's imperious wife appeared frequently on TV.

It wasn't yet nine o'clock, yet she was gripping a can of Diet Coke. "Are you Dario?" she asked, waving in my face a famous

credit-card company's magazine; it was a special edition dedicated entirely to Italy. "Where are you taking us today?"

I explained, without going into detail, that we would be
exploring the Chianti area, straying a bit from the normal tourist
routes. Her face fell in disappointment. "That means we won't
make it to Veneto!" She flipped open the magazine to a page on
which a shoe store on the outskirts of Venice was written up. I
pointed out that Venice was at least a five-hour drive from Siena
and that therefore it was absolutely out of the question.

"Okay," she said, flipping through the magazine, "we can go
to Ponte di Legno." She opened it to a page promoting a store
that specialized in lace. "It's in Lucca, that's close to Tuscany!" I
gently explained that Tuscany is very large, and that Lucca is
completely outside the areas in which I operate.

She was undaunted. "Fine, no Lucca," she said, again flipping pages, "but for lunch you have to take us to La
Bruschetta"—and here she displayed a page giving top marks to
a restaurant I knew to be terrible. I glared at the magazine, sens-
ing that its authority was repeatedly going to challenge my own.
I had a sudden urge to grab it and rip it to pieces.

I tried convincing her that it would be far too complicated
to tour Chianti in the morning and then dash all the way to that
particular restaurant for lunch—omitting that fact that the quality of its food would make it an even greater waste of time. She
was unyielding. Fortunately we were interrupted by the arrival
of her husband and the husband of my old client. My old client
herself, however, remained absent, so that after a while the two
men started to quarrel.

"Always the same old story; your wife holds us up!"

"Well, you knew what she was like when you agreed to
come along."

The squabble continued, with no attempt even to mute its volume for my benefit, and I began feeling a bit uneasy. Finally the organizer arrived. Her eyelashes were marred by tiny clumps of mascara and her lipstick was a bit smudged, as though she had put her makeup on in a hurry.

Finally, after this half-hour delay, we all climbed into the mini van. The two men sat stiffly silent after their quarrel; my client's friend paged angrily through her magazine, upset at my lack of cooperation; and my client herself kept making embarrassed apologies for the delay. To ease the tension I began telling them what was ahead. "I'll be taking you on a full-immersion tour of Chianti. We'll visit two wineries, one ancient and small, the other modern and large; some medieval villages; and a famous castle. We'll stop for lunch in a typical restaurant managed by a local family. But first, we'll explore an Etruscan archaeological site." I then began my introductory spiel on the history and culture of Chianti territory.

Immediately "Mirjana" interrupted me. "Dario, as an alternative to the archaeological site, where else could you take us? I'm really not interested in Etruscans." Taken aback, I asked if she knew anything about Etruscan history. The answer was loud, clear, and unashamed. "No, I've never heard of them, never read about them, and have no intention of learning anything about them now."

I suggested that some knowledge of the Etruscan people was crucial to understanding the history of Tuscany, and that since the others seemed game, we'd stick to our original plan. Without waiting for her to reply, I launched into a narration on the Etruscans, explaining why I considered them so important.

Once again she interrupted me. "Why don't you tell us something about the Palio instead?" As it happens, the Palio of

Siena—the semiannual bareback horse race held in the city's central piazza—is one of my passions. But I was reserving that discussion for the following day, when I promised I would tell them all about its history and pageantry, as well as show them a video of the actual event. Mirjana laughed derisively, and in a presumptuous tone exclaimed, "I certainly haven't come all the way to Italy to watch a video."

"Okay, no video," I said, just to see if it was possible to please her in some way. In the meantime we'd arrived at the archaeological site. As we got out of the van, we could feel that the temperature had risen, so most of the group doffed their jackets. Mirjana, however, remained firmly layered in her heavy ensemble.

We made our way to the site and I took them through the dig, explaining the findings and elaborating on their importance. While we were still inside the main tomb, the largest and most spectacular, I asked if anyone had any questions. Mirjana had one: "Ever been married?" Her husband was also quick to ask, "How far is Positano from here?"

Demoralized, I said that Positano was approximately six hours by car, and that no, I had never been married, and I never would be if all wives were this unbearable—though I kept this last thought to myself.

On the path through the cypresses that took us back to the car, they told me that they'd rented a car to go to Positano, but now they thought maybe they'd prefer to be driven. It seemed to me a good idea, so using my cell phone I called the rental agency and canceled their car, then found them a driver to take them where they wished to go.

The men seemed satisfied with this arrangement. During the next stage of our tour, however, at the first of our two vineyards,

Mirjana turned to me in the middle of the tasting and asked me to cancel the reservation with the driver and reorder the rental car. A bit embarrassed, I made the calls. I then pointed out to the group that the rental employees had graciously consented to be in the office to serve them, despite it being a national holiday.

At the end of the lunch, during which Mirjana refused to drink wine but drained three Diet Cokes, we went to a ceramics store she insisted on visiting. (I have no doubt it was recommended by The Magazine.) After having dragged us away from our set program to get there, after having touched each item and driven the store clerks half crazy, she left without buying a thing. Next up: Castle Brolio. During the walk around the imposing medieval walls, the party of four continued to discuss the Positano matter until, arriving at the point where the foliage opens to reveal a spectacular panorama of the Chianti countryside—one of the highlights of my tours, which invariably takes clients' breath away—the group completely ignored the vista and instead asked me to recancel the rental car and reengage the driver. Disturbed by their complete lack of consideration for the people involved, I made the two hateful telephone calls, then told them, "Please, this must be the last time!"

After the tour concluded I left them at the hotel they had reserved for that night and, as I'd agreed, returned to the previous one to pick up their luggage. I was feeling rather pent up and needed to talk to someone about what I'd just been through, so I stopped for a word with the concierge. He seemed to be in even greater distress than I was. "Imagine it," he said. "They reserved the royal suite"—the one in greatest demand because its four picture windows provide a 360-degree view of the landscape—"but one of the women . . . the one dressed like a Russian *maîtresse* . . . didn't like it. According to her, there was 'too much light.' If that's not a room to thrill anybody, I need to change careers."

I comforted the poor guy, telling him that at least he wouldn't be saddled with them any longer, while I had them for yet another day. I asked if he could show me to their luggage. He smirked, then took me to a storage room stacked with suitcases, bags, beauty cases, trunks, boxes, and various other containers of all shapes and sizes. Thinking this must be the luggage depository for the entire hotel, I said, "Okay, which are theirs?"

He grinned cruelly. "All of them."

I was unable to reply.

I lowered the seats in my van and loaded the baggage so as to fill up each atom of available space with scientific precision. It took me some time to do so. En route to the new hotel, it occurred to me that this amount of luggage could easily serve for a world tour of several years' duration. When I reached the hotel, I unloaded everything onto the curb as the staff looked on in disbelief. I then spoke to the receptionist, to offer a word of friendly warning, but it was too late—by the pale, beaten look on his face, I could tell he'd already made acquaintance with Mirjana. I left, glad to be free of them but dreading the following day.

That night I dreamed that I was beleaguered by people with bizarre and impossible requests, and while I was working to fulfill them, they changed their minds and wanted the opposite, equally bizarre and equally impossible. When I awoke I knew it was to a reality that would be no different.

As I pulled up to the hotel, I was surprised to find the two couples already waiting for me, but even more surprised that despite having enough suitcases to dress an Elton John concert tour, they were all wearing exactly the same clothes as the day before. Even Mirjana was swaddled in the same snug wool suit.

Our schedule for the day comprised a drive to the Monastery of Monte Oliveto Maggiore to admire the splendid medieval frescoes painted by Luca Signorelli and Antonio Bazzi, better known as Il Sodoma; a panoramic drive through the lunar landscapes in the Crete area; a stop in Montalcino to visit a producer of the world-famous Brunello wine; and, as a grand finale, an hour at Sant'Antimo, a gorgeous Romanesque church built by Charlemagne in the year 800, nestled deep in the Tuscan countryside, where we would listen to the resident monks lift their celestial voices in Gregorian chant.

When I ran through these plans for my customers, Mirjana said she had no intention of listening to any Gregorian chants. She considered them too "commercial." Back in the States, she insisted, she could hear them anytime she wanted—why, the church at the corner of her street "put them on" every evening. For the first time in many years, instead of the compliments and enthusiasm, I was being asked for a list of alternatives to Sant'Antimo. By this point the other passengers were feeling some embarrassment and tried to come to my aid, but since Mirjana seemed intransigent, they had to reach a compromise. We would go to Sant'Antimo to hear the chants, but we would leave Mirjana in Montalcino, whose shopping was recommended by The Magazine. We would pick her up after the chanting concluded.

I agreed to the plan, knowing full well that it was a holiday and the stores would not be open.

During an exquisite lunch at Giovanni's, the proprietor himself—a kind of amalgam of Luciano Pavarotti and Henry VIII— paid us special attention despite having a full house, entertaining us with his patented routine of jokes and gags. Giovanni's menu offered typical Tuscan dishes: *crostini*, salamis, and *bruschette* for antipasti; *pici*, tagliatelle, minestrone, and *pasta e ceci* for first-course choices; grilled meats, rabbit cooked in Brunello, and guinea fowl for the second course; and, for dessert, a long list of homemade cakes. Every single plate was cooked with ingredients grown locally, including the meats and the game.

For some reason I never did manage to learn, the two men started quarreling again, with even greater animosity than before; and this time the wives joined in, yelling at each other across the table and ruining the peaceful atmosphere in the restaurant. Demoralized and thoroughly embarrassed, I endeavored to ignore the situation to the extent possible and decided at the very least to enjoy an extra glass of the great 1990 *riserva* we'd ordered. Giovanni, seeing that I was in a difficult situation, even offered me a shot of his best grappa—the one he only serves to his most cherished customers.

By the end of lunch, they had all somehow made peace. Before continuing to Sant'Antimo, we dropped Mirjana off in Montalcino. I don't know if it was the effect of the wine and the grappa, or the absence of Mirjana, or both, but the chanting seemed even more serenely harmonious than usual, and restored my sense of peace.

We returned to Montalcino for Mirjana. Despite the extreme warmth of the day, she was still wrapped tight in her wool suit, by now soiled with two horrible sweat stains under her arms. Evidently the fear of breaking up her ensemble was enough to induce her to brave any temperature.

She was furious because the few stores she'd found had all been closed. But not wishing to dwell on the unflattering fact that she'd made a wrong choice, she immediately whipped out

The Magazine, by now a kind of bible to her; she was determined to steer us to our next triumph, which she'd read about while waiting for us to return for her.

"'Close to Montalcino,'" she read aloud, "'is a Romanesque church situated in a valley of olives and cypresses, where in spring hundreds of brightly colored wildflowers bloom. It was constructed partly in granite and partly in alabaster from local quarries, and represents one of the most imposing examples of Romanesque art in the Mediterranean. Legend has it that it was constructed in a single night by fairies, but we know it was really erected during the Frankish domination of Italy. Today it is inhabited by a small group of young French friars whose splendid plainsong you will be able to hear if you have the good fortune to arrive in the hours dedicated to their prayers.'" She looked up, beaming. "The church is called Sant'Antimo. Do you know where it is? I'd like to see it."

I paused to savor the moment. Then, trying to mask my enormous satisfaction, I told her that Sant'Antimo was exactly where we'd just been.

Her face did a slow burn, and she tried to laugh off the matter, making some absurd comment that even so, she hadn't regretted her decision. Still, it was clear that she was deeply embarrassed and disappointed.

I delivered them to the third hotel they'd booked and went again to collect their luggage. Transporting that mountain of stuff was no easier the second time around. By the time I finished unloading, the hour was rather late, so I went to say goodbye to the two couples, delighted that my time with them was over. Very kindly they thanked me for having arranged their driver for the next day, and even apologized for all the trouble they'd caused with their indecision.

As I was leaving, Mirjana's husband took me aside, gave me a very generous tip, and said, "My wife is so pretty and sweet, don't you think?" I was taken aback; in the two days I'd known her, I'd come up with quite a few adjectives to describe her, but these were not among them. All the same, I answered, "Very pretty and sweet indeed." He smiled brightly. I think he'd needed to hear me say it for him to be able to believe it himself.

On the way home I stopped for a celebratory drink. Sipping a glass of Prosecco, I vowed to myself, *The next time someone says my job must be so much fun, and how lucky I am to be able to meet so many interesting people, I will strangle him.*

The next day, by sheer chance, I ran into the driver I'd arranged to take the group to Positano. Astonished, I said, "What are you doing in Siena? Shouldn't you be on the road with my clients by now?" He said he'd gone to their hotel that morning to pick them up, but they'd already departed with another service booked by the hotel.

I noticed that he was miffed by this, and he was clearly awaiting my apology. I left him without making one. Why should I? He didn't know it, but it had been his lucky day.

THE FIRST EXCURSION

Suddenly, after three months of excruciating silence, the miracle occurred. In mid-May an Englishman called me from a hotel in Florence. He introduced himself as "Vesey" and said, "I've just seen your brochure, and was wondering if it would be possible for you to organize something for my wife and me tomorrow. So sorry about the late notice. Understand if you can't." I started shaking, so much so that it required both hands to keep the phone to my ear while I replied, "Of course, sir," in a pronounced upper-class British accent.

We quickly agreed on logistics: I would pick them up the next morning at nine o'clock at their hotel. When I lowered the phone, I was ecstatic, but soon a wave of panic washed over me. *My God*, I thought, *will I really be up to it? Will they have any interest at all in the places I want to show them? Will I be able to answer any of their questions? What if they're bored?*

I was so worried about first impressions that I rushed into the courtyard to wash the car—perhaps a little too zealously. By the time I finished, it had the antiseptic scent of an ambulance. I then returned to the house and started boning up on the history of Chianti, as though I had some important exam the following day. I was as taut as a violin string. That night I set the alarm for 4:30 A.M., so frightened was I that I might oversleep and arrive late for my very first clients. In any case I scarcely slept at all and got up before the alarm went off. When I left the house, it was still dark, and I arrived in Florence a full three hours early. I parked in front of the hotel and started feverishly rereading my notes, puffing one cigarette after another.

Finally the fateful hour arrived. With my heart beating in my ears, I introduced myself to the receptionist and said that I had an appointment with the Veseys. At nine o'clock sharp my first two customers appeared and put themselves into my care. Mrs. Vesey wore a long flowery dress and a Queen Mother–style hat; she carried a tiny handbag not large enough for even a packet of tissues. She seemed to be somewhere in her forties. Her husband, however, was much older, around seventy, and very distinguished in his khaki safari suit. They struck me at once as the typical, agreeable English couple you'd expect to find at any British garden party.

After shaking hands we left the hotel. They observed my little egg-shaped van with a moment's curiosity, then gamely entered it, both climbing into the backseat. (In the future I tried to steer my customers away from this, because it made me feel more like a chauffeur than a tour guide.) As we pulled away from the hotel, I told them a little about my childhood in London. They listened appreciatively, and with the ice now broken, we settled in for the long drive.

It was a splendid mid-May morning; the sky was an intense blue, the sun was riding high in the sky, and the air was as limpid as any tourist could desire. I couldn't have asked for better.

The roads were another matter. Leaving Florence can often be problematic because of the intense traffic, and being Italian I usually drive without bothering too much about the speed limit. On this day, however, I sat straight in my seat, both hands firmly gripping the steering wheel, and heeded every single road sign that came my way. I was not about to terrify my very first customers.

I explained to the Veseys that as a consequence of an ancient medieval rivalry, I didn't much like going to Florence. I told them how we Sienese continue to taunt the Florentines about the major defeat they suffered at our hands on September 4, 1260, the mere mention of which can still cause Florentines of any age to wince in discomfort. Crossing the bridge over the Arno, I also explained that in 1966 the river broke the banks, almost completely flooding the city, and that in Siena we are always cheering on the river and wishing it better luck next time. Seeing the Veseys' stricken faces, I hastened to add that this was a joke—obviously no one really hopes for a disaster of such magnitude to recur, especially considering the number of artworks that were ruined. The Veseys visibly relaxed at this reassurance.

Once out of Florence, we took the SS 222, passing the American World War II cemetery and memorial as well as the area's terra-cotta factories. Finally we entered Chianti. We sailed by Greve, native city of Amerigo Vespucci and Giovanni di Verrazano, then up the rolling hills for a spectacular view of the *rinascimentale* Villa Vignamaggio, where, legend has it, Leonardo painted *La Gioconda*, immortalizing the villa's owner, Mona Lisa Gherardini. (In more recent times the villa was used as the setting for Kenneth Branagh's film version of *Much Ado About Nothing*.) From there the road continued its winding ascent, with tight and harrowing turns that I took as carefully as possible, until we reached the charming village of Panzano. Here I turned off the main thoroughfare and continued on one of my beloved gravelly "white roads." As we ambled along at low speed, I endeavored to entertain my clients with every historical, geographical, and oenological detail I could recall about the territory, resulting in such an authoritative flow of patter that I impressed even myself. Mrs. Vesey was particularly struck by the masses of colorful wildflowers she surveyed from the immaculate windows, especially the poppies, which looked like they'd burst straight from one of the unruly fields in a Van Gogh painting.

Crossing the provincial border, I said with a wink that we were now safe, since we were no longer in enemy territory but in the Sienese part of Chianti. After a few more miles on this panoramic road, slicing through thick forests of firs and chestnuts, we pulled into the tiny village of Volpaia, inhabited by about fifty souls and some thirty dogs. The village was originally an ancient medieval fort and only much later, after Siena and Florence finally made peace in 1555, transformed into a village. It still retains evidence of its military origins, with its massive stone structures and its main tower turned vigilantly south.

Volpaia is chiefly known for its famous winery, whose functions are distributed all over the village. Practically every other room on the ground floor of each building is a cellar, an office, or has something else to do with the business. After a short walk, on which I outlined the area's entire history with the precision of an academic, we sat in the village's only bar and refreshed ourselves with a Campari and gin each.

Back in the car, we descended the hill toward the valley, detouring on another of my secret back roads, this one taking us through an acacia forest. The Veseys were thus the first people I escorted to the series of Etruscan tombs dug on a little hill hidden inside a natural cypress grove. These four tombs, dating from approximately 700 B.C., had only recently been discovered, and have given us additional insights into the people to whom we attribute the basis of our culture.

All was proceeding wonderfully. My two clients seemed delighted by the tour thus far, and perhaps also by my youth, shyness, and extreme deference. I was behaving more like a Buckingham Palace page than a tour guide; I might as well have rolled out a red carpet at every stop.

The next stop was at the winery where I had worked for seven years. I was a bit nervous about reappearing here in my new role of tour guide, and in fact I squirmed beneath the sly grins and snickers of my former colleagues as they observed me squiring about this pair of upper-class British tourists. I could only imagine the comments made behind my back.

That said, I will never be able to adequately thank the Cecchi family for opening their doors to me. Wineries in Italy are not traditionally accessible to visitors, the way they are in France or California. Because of my long association and friendship with the family, however, the Cecchis graciously allowed me this privilege. The Cecchi winery, founded in 1893, is a fine example of a family-run business, successfully handed down from father to son for several generations. Originally it sold large quantities of bulk wine, but over the years it has evolved and enlarged its production, always in keeping with the times, and today, with its modern system of vinification and its high-tech bottling lines, it produces and exports millions of high-quality bottles all over the world.

Despite all the sardonic grins, my return as an outsider to the building where I had worked from age fifteen also had for me the sweet taste of victory. Having left the life of a laborer now seemed not so much a tumble down the social ladder as a step onto an escalator, destination: paradise. The visit lasted approximately an hour, during which I supplied the Veseys with a short history of the region's wine, explaining how Chianti Classico is created and other variations on this topic. They seemed astounded by the dimensions of the stainless-steel vats and oaken barrels in the underground cellars, and flabbergasted by the sophisticated bottling equipment capable of filling, labeling, and corking thousands of bottles an hour. Obviously, having been surrounded by all that gushing wine, we couldn't resist a little tasting. We each drew a glass directly from an open barrel, and after having sipped and praised Bacchus's finest returned to the car.

For lunch I'd chosen a small trattoria in a village called Fonterutoli. The Grey Cat, owned by a good friend of mine, has an excellent menu, though the locals frown a bit at the young "alternative" customers its reputation draws. We ordered Tuscan *crostini* as a starter; then I had some tagliatelle with hare sauce, Mrs. Vesey a bread and tomato soup, and Mr. Vesey some home-made angel-hair spaghetti served with an unusual lemon sauce. We washed it all down with a vintage Chianti Classico. For the second course we decided on a tray of grilled meats composed of pork ribs, chicken, and sausages, accompanied by a robust local wine called Concerto, produced in the vineyards that encircled the restaurant. We finished by soaking *cantuccini* biscuits in a mellow *vin santo*. After the coffee the host offered us a round of grappa that we gladly accepted.

Refreshed and happy, I paid the bill and ushered my clients out of the tiny restaurant to continue the tour. Our next stop was a small winery close to Radda in Chianti, owned by an Italian but managed by a German. The property, situated at the top of a hill, was indeed splendid. Both the house and the wine cellar have been restored beautifully, with every detail obsessively seen to; not one blade of grass was out of place. The main objective of the stop was to visit the owner's private museum, a collection of timeworn objects, tools, and curiosities that had belonged to the old peasants' world. Here, unfortunately, things didn't work out as I'd hoped; although I had made very precise arrangements, they didn't allow us to visit the museum but took advantage of my presence to hand me over to an entire busload of German tourists, all in need of various kinds of information.

My customers, of course, weren't at all pleased by the intrusion, nor by the failed attempt to see the museum. The combination of this class-conscious English couple and a loud, rude group of Germans was already a prickly one without the Veseys' added astonishment at seeing a German running a farm here in Tuscany. These annoyances, however, could not withstand the calming effect of some excellent red wines, which we later sampled directly from the oaken barrels that surrounded the walls of the aging cellar.

Mr. Vesey actually bought a few bottles, and it was at this point that I discovered—by a chance glimpse at the contents of his wallet—that he wasn't Mr. Vesey at all. He was Lord Vesey. I was rather glad I hadn't known this till now; it might have made my first-client jitters just that much more unmanageable.

During the drive back to Florence, Lord Vesey, now completely inebriated, fell asleep with his head on his wife's shoulder and started snoring loudly. Lady Vesey, whom I'm sure must have ached to join him in a well-earned doze, nevertheless maintained her English aplomb and remained wide awake and composed for the entire drive.

I delivered them to their hotel at around five o'clock. They insisted I join them for a glass of beer at the hotel bar, and when we sat down they told me what a wonderful day they'd had. They predicted that within a few years I would need a whole fleet of mini buses to handle all the requests I'd have for Chianti tours, while I would sit comfortably in an office overseeing it all. I was immensely flattered and at the same time very embarrassed; and you can imagine how I squirmed when they insisted on calling over the hotel director to recommend my services to his other customers. They left me their business card, invited me to go and visit them in London, and gave me a generous tip.

On the drive home I was euphoric; even the inevitable Florentine traffic jam couldn't dampen my mood. I began to shout—nothing in particular at first, just some inarticulate animal noises that allowed me both to express my great joy and to relieve the day's tension. (The not insignificant amount of alcohol I'd imbibed may also have had something to do with it.)

"I made it, I made it!" I howled happily. "I'll be able to make millions!"

Later, back at home, I added up the expenses and compared them to my fee. I was in for quite a shock. After the cost of gas, the lunch bill, the drinks, and the taxes, I was about a hundred dollars in the red—and this despite the large tip. I couldn't believe it was possible and recounted three times, hoping to find some obvious but enormous mistake. Each time, the result was the same.

I was becoming rapidly aware of the difficulties of conducting a tour like the one I'd just completed. And there was more than just the expense to consider: If entertaining two people for the better part of each day, with all the attendant eating, drinking, and smoking, didn't ruin my finances, it would surely ruin my health. Perhaps it was better to reorganize the tour, adding more historical sites at the expense of a few of the wine tastings.

As it turned out, I had plenty of time to think about it, because the Veseys were the only Chianti Rooster Tours customers for that entire season. I managed to survive the remainder of the year by taking odd jobs. I worked as a bricklayer, a waiter, and a grape picker; I even taught English to children. Through it all I never abandoned my dream, and every time I came across a new hotel, I stopped and left a packet of brochures. Thanks to the Veseys and their kind words, I was more determined than ever to carry on.

JULY AND THE PALIO

Sunshine! And with it the time to devote to long, lazy meditations in the garden, while observing the ongoing comedy of nature. The lizards are everywhere, each one lord of its own small domain. In the torpid stillness two begin a sudden squabble that degenerates into mortal combat, until a light noise distracts them and they dart away in opposite directions. A pair of butterflies indulge in an aerial dance, so nimbly and gracefully that it's difficult to imagine their previous lives as sluggish caterpillars. Another lizard is pursued by a snake, both of them too busy to notice a nearby human presence. Watching them disappear beneath a clump of hollyhocks, I worry about the fate of the lizard—it being only natural to root for the underdog. Then an enormous yellow-green lizard appears—briefly, as though making a royal visit. He beams with reptilian self-satisfaction, somehow aware of his exceptional beauty. Not far away, a large snake tries to enter a very small crack. It seems impossible that he can manage it, but inch by inch he squeezes himself in until he's gone. It's funny to think how many guests of mine have sat on that precise spot. One final glance takes in the ants, stolidly bearing such enormous cargoes on their wiry shoulders—exemplars of lives devoted to joyless duty. But now the eyelids droop and sleep prevails. In July, in Chianti, the siesta is a vital necessity.

In the deep of the night, I am summoned by the telephone. Still half asleep, I raise the receiver and hear a determined voice: "Hallo, am I speaking to Dario?"

"Yes, speaking," I reply, freeing myself from the arms of Morpheus.

The man has a twangy Texan accent and is obviously unaware of the time difference. "Listen, Dario, could you organize a mini Palio for my wife? We're not in Italy for real long, so we won't be able to see the main one. And you know, she just loves horses so much." In more than ten years of outlandish requests from my customers, this is the most bizarre I've yet encountered. On the subject of the Palio, entire books could be (and have been!) written. A guide can, as I do, give lectures, show videos, drill the lore of the event into outsiders' heads— even take visitors to the race itself. But no one outside the walls of Siena will ever succeed in fully understanding and appreciating the real meaning of this remarkable spectacle, which has been the pinnacle of Siena's civil and social year since the Middle Ages.

Roughly, this is what it's all about:

Like all medieval cities, Siena was divided into districts, which we call *contrade*. Each *contrada* represented a distinct zone of the city and had an independent life, including its own public square, church, and fountain, as though it were a small village, and in each such "village" the inhabitants belonged to a guild. The first rivalries started when the borders of these territories were traced, and this explains why a *contrada's* rival district is usually the one next door. Each *contrada* also had its own army; during the numerous wars against Florence, in the case of a sudden attack, it was easier to organize many small armies than pull together a large one under a single command. Even today the *contrada* maintains an organization with a military charter stamp, with rigid rules and hierarchies.

During long sieges the Sienese gathered in public squares and organized games in which physical clashes were preferred. The *elmora*, a false combat between two divisions with wooden weapons and wicker shields, was one of them, eventually banned because it was too violent. Another was the *giorgiano*, where a group of armed men with blunt swords had to defend a fort from the assault of another group. This was suspended when it failed to find favor with the public. The public did, however, adore the game of the *pugna*, which was played from 1261 through the first years of the eighteenth century. This was a kind of combat without weapons; the fighting consisted of punches, slaps, and sometimes even bites.

The *pallonata* was a ball game played on the feast day of Saint Stephen. Two teams faced each other in the Campo, or town square. To start the game the ball was launched from the top of the town hall tower, upon which the teams would immediately begin slugging, pushing, and tripping their opponents in an attempt to force the ball into the adversary's goal, constituted by two streets' entrances. Despite the free-for-all, almost hooligan nature of the game, it was, like medieval jousting tournaments, reserved for noble knights.

Bullfights began in 1499 under the Spanish influence and established the foundation for the Palio in that these matches were the first in which the *contrade* participated as opponents. Then in 1599 the *contrade* began to race in the Campo; but they raced oxen, not horses. At the end of a procession in which the guilds flaunted their civic pride, the beasts were made to run three turns around the square. To the *contrada* of the winning ox

Contrada	Flag	Victories in the Past Century	Rival Contrada
The Caterpillar (Noble Contrada)	Green, yellow, and blue	5	none
The Dragon	Red and green	16	none
The Eagle (Noble Contrada)	Yellow and black with blue	11	The Panther
The Forest	Green and orange with white	14	none
The Giraffe (Imperial Contrada)	Red and white	15	none
The Goose (Noble Contrada)	Green, red, and white	20	The Tower
The Mutton	Red and yellow with white	15	The Shell
The Owl (Prior Contrada)	Red and black	8	The Unicorn
The Panther	Red and blue with white	9	The Eagle
The Porcupine (Sovereign Contrada)	Blue, white, black, and red	9	The She-wolf
The Shell (Noble Contrada)	Blue with red and yellow	16	The Mutton
The She-wolf	Black and white with orange	11	The Porcupine
The Snail	Red and yellow	14	The Turtle
The Tower	Crimson	5	The Goose and the Wave
The Turtle	Yellow and blue	12	The Snail
The Unicorn	Orange and white with blue	10	The Owl
The Wave (Contrada Capitana)	Light blue and white	11	The Tower

was given the Palio, a woven piece of precious cloth. The ox that had performed most impressively in the procession was awarded a sculpture called the Masgalano.

Later on were organized the *asinate* (donkey races) and a race with horses, called "at the long" because it was run along the city streets, without jockeys. And thus we arrive at the modern event.

The Palio is run in the Campo twice each summer: on July 2, in honor of the Madonna of Provenzano, and on August 16, in honor of the Madonna Assunta. The first date was institutionalized in 1659, the second in 1774. With the edict of Princess Violante of Bavaria in 1729, the *contrade* themselves became institutionalized, their borders officially drawn and their number reduced from twenty-three to the current seventeen. The Rooster, the Viper, the Bear, the Lion, the Strong Sword, and the Oak were consigned to history.

One of the questions I'm asked most frequently is how a person becomes a member of a *contrada*. There is no simple answer. The easiest way is to be a native Sienese; if you are born inside the city walls, you will automatically be baptized in your *contrada* of residence. Thus it can happen—and indeed it happens very often—that family members will belong to different *contrade*, even to the point of children embracing different colors from those of their parents because they have been born in different parts of the city. But it isn't enough to have been born in a *contrada* to be able to style yourself *contradaiolo*. The *contrada* is in reality a big family, and as such it has traditions and rituals that must be respected, followed, and attended to. There are thousands of duties to perform, assemblies to attend, festivities to organize, and marches to march. The young *contradaioli* must be taught the arts of drumming and flag twirling; the elderly must be provided for and looked after. From a sociological point of view, *contrada* life is virtually unique in the modern world—a kind of benevolent urban tribalism. In Siena minor crime is almost nonexistent, and the people live a serene life filled with civic activities. The only negative aspect is that the microcosmos of the *contrade* make Siena a rather closed city, its society difficult for outsiders to penetrate. (But as I will show in a later chapter, if you have will and patience, it is possible even for a foreigner to become a valued part of it.)

Each *contrada* has a headquarters that functions not only as a base of operations but also as a museum and recreational facility. The head of the *contrada* is the prior, who is assisted by a vicar, a *camerlengo*, a *bilanciere*, an *economo*, one or more *vice economi*, a chancellor, a vice chancellor, an archivist, and finally a captain who represents the *contrada* in the Palio.

Other arms of the *contrada* are the general assembly and the council of the people. *Contrada* titles are elective and can be renewed at various times; the *contradaioli* can vote as long as they are older than eighteen. Anyone in the *contrada* can hold office; there is no discrimination based on gender, occupation, or economic condition. In fact, the only place in *contrada* life in which discrimination exists is the historical parade before the Palio, and this is simply because the event is a reenactment of the military parades of the medieval era, in which women (not being soldiers) did not participate.

Although the term *Palio* has become synonymous with the horse race, in actuality it refers to the painted standard awarded to the victorious *contrada*. Since the entire event is dedicated to the Madonna, the Palio must incorporate an image of the Virgin Mary, as well as the colors of the participating *contrade*. Beyond that—and certain dimensions to which the cloth must adhere—

the appearance of the Palio is left entirely to the imagination of the artist. Painters are selected from both within Siena and the outside world; some have had international reputations.

The first big event of the Palio season is the drawing of the *contrade*, held approximately a month before each race. Since there isn't room in the Campo for all seventeen *contrade* to race, only ten participate. Each July, the seven that did not run the previous July are automatically placed on the roster, with the remaining three places filled by a drawing of names from the remaining ten. The same rules apply for the August Palio. In this way the two races are distinct and separate events. It's possible, in fact, that a *contrada* particularly blessed by luck can run twice the same year—though it will then be excluded from both races the year following, unless by chance its name is drawn.

On the Sunday of the lottery, the windows on the town hall facade are hung with the seven flags of the participating *contrade*. As the names of three additional *contrade* are drawn, their flags are added. The actual drawing is performed by the mayor and the captains, while in the square itself an enormous crowd waits with bated breath for the hoisting of the three chosen flags—at the sight of which the *contradaioli* of the lucky *contrade* explode with joy and burst into repeated, rapturous choruses of their *contrada's* anthem.

The activity in the *contrade* suddenly becomes frenetic. Hymns echo through the hidden alleys of the old city; the city's phone lines buzz with arrangements and organizing; and on the square, bleachers rise up to obscure the storefronts, while the perimeter of the Campo is overlaid with earth.

If the lottery represents the opening of the festivity, the transformation of the public square into a racetrack signals the true beginning of the Palio. In the evening the Sienese are drawn to the Campo, to tread happily on the track, to lounge on the uncomfortable bleachers, and, as always, to sing. Anticipation begins to build, and does not abate until the race.

Four days before the Palio (June 29 and August 13), the final lineup of horses, each of which has undergone strict selection processes and exhaustive veterinary testing, is determined. After a series of test runs, the captains choose the ten that will actually run the Palio. The choice is made around one o'clock; in the meantime thousands of hopeful *contradaioli* gather in the Campo. The ten horses are usually chosen to make the race exciting. Two or three will be big names—those that have previously won the Palio. Another two or three will have run without winning. The others will be Palio debutantes. The horses are placed in wooden stalls before the magnificent town hall building. At the blare of a trumpet, the ten captains and the mayor exit the hall and take their place on a raised platform. Nearby, the representatives of the *contrade*—each in costume—stand waiting. The crowd, rather unfairly, holds them responsible for the result of the drawing: If a *contrada* is awarded a good horse, its representative will be overwhelmed by kisses and embraces by his fellows; if not, his reception will be much less felicitous.

The mayor draws the name of a horse for each *contrada*. Of all the phases of the Palio, this is perhaps the moment that I love most: The sustained outbreaks of joy among those *contradaioli* lucky enough to get a good horse can verge on the hysterical. The initial roar of surprise and delight washes over me like a wave, and when the *contradaioli* go and fetch the animal and bring it into the square, singing wildly with their fists raised in the air, goose bumps are the order of the day.

And yet there is also desperation; there are pockets of stunned silence; there is the dismay of the *contrada* awarded by cruel fate a less desirable mount. It's not uncommon to see grown men cry, even as they exit the Campo with their heads held high. And it is at this moment that the teasing begins—the taunts and mocking songs directed by the fortunate *contrade* against those less so. It's usually in good fun, but *contrada* loyalty can only be provoked so far, and occasionally the name-calling degenerates into a healthy fistfight.

The horses, of course, are removed from any such anarchy. Each is installed within its new *contrada*, in a stable so clean and well appointed that it can look more like an elegant living room. The member in charge of the horse (the *barbaresco*) will in fact actually live there, sharing the stable with the animal until the day of the Palio. You can't be too careful . . .

As soon as the drawing ends comes the moment for the jockeys, whom we call "assassins." The most controversial figures of the Palio, they are the true mercenaries of the event. It's rare that they remain loyal to a *contrada*. Originally the jockeys were Sienese, but after the mass emigration of the shepherds from the island of Sardinia in the 1960s, Sardinians began to infiltrate the ranks, and today they hold a virtual monopoly on the job. Perhaps this is because they are on the whole a smaller people, or perhaps because they traditionally excel in bareback riding. Still, whatever the reason, they have continually proven themselves the best.

Every *contrada* tries to have a jockey under contract, even if neither the *contrada* nor the jockey is likely to respect the agreement very far. By his own choice or at the decision of the *contrada*, the jockey can go and race for other colors.

The choice of the jockey is a logical consequence of the drawing of the horse: A good horse attracts an equally famous jockey. It can happen that a jockey who has raced often for the same *contrada* can decide to go and race for the enemy. Never trust the jockey! He may even be capable of taking payment from his own *contrada* to win at the same time he's accepting a bribe from the enemy to lose.

With the addition of the jockeys to the picture, strategies begin in earnest. In order to win a Palio, it's necessary to have a lot of luck, but it's equally important to have a captain capable of making the right alliances. For example, a *contrada* that hasn't won for many years may obtain a good horse and a good jockey, but it will sweeten its odds by paying another *contrada*, recently victorious and with a bad horse, to help it out—by giving way at the start, obstructing a favorite horse assigned to a rival, or the like. These negotiations are, of course, conducted in great secrecy, day and night, right up to the last moment before the race begins. Even the *contrade* that aren't racing will get in on the scheming, to try to prevent their rivals from achieving victory—often, if necessary, offering money to the rival's jockey. In the gossip-filled weeks before the Palio, I find it vastly entertaining to listen to the thousands of possibilities and speculations everyone has regarding bribes and strategies. Considering the energy put into the constant talk itself, I sometimes wonder whether any will be left over to make this great underground movement happen at all!

But you shouldn't wonder at all this frantic plotting and counterplotting; the stakes, after all, are very high. More than the World Cup, more than Hollywood, in Siena the Palio functions as our modern mythology. Even the horses are heroes. Many have become legends and entered the hearts of the Sienese for having won particularly brilliant victories: Brandano Rimini, Panezio, and Phiteos are steeds that will never be forgotten. In Siena the horse is seen as a sacred animal and treated with extraordinary care. It's true that during the race they will occasionally, unfortunately, be hurt; but such incidents happen in all events in which horses race.

The jockeys, too, take their place in history. A name above all others is Andrea De Gortes, known as "Vinegar," who won an incredible fourteen Palios. Even so, the jockeys are never truly loved. Indeed, it often happens that at the end of a race, a jockey is attacked and beaten by the *contradaioli* who hired him, and who are not entirely appreciative of his performance.

Between the afternoon of the drawing and the morning of the Palio, the jockeys test the horses, racing them in the public square six times. These trials are important mainly to give the horses familiarity and confidence—not only with the starting gate and the earthen track, but also with the thousands of wildly excited spectators pressing in on the track from all sides.

Before each trial a stirring and emotional ritual occurs: The *barbaresco* leads the horse to the Campo, followed by hundreds of the *contradaioli* singing their anthem, often adding new, offensive lyrics directed toward their rival.

When all the *contrade* have so marched in and filled the Campo, the trials begin. The starting line is placed close to the main entrance of the square, where a contraption called a *verrocchio* is installed. This is operated by the starter (the *mossiere*), who holds a large rope taut across the track by means of a winch placed beyond the fence. A few yards behind this rope—called the *canapo*—is another, shorter rope that allows space for the entrance of the horses. Next to the winch, a firecracker sits in a cage atop a pole; this will be the signal for the trial (and later the race) to begin.

At every trial, and on the day of the Palio itself, the positions of the horses inside the *canapi* are selected. It isn't until the first nine are aligned in place that the tenth, the *di rincorsa* (literally "runner-up"), starts the race by entering the *canapi*. This apparently simple operation can take ages because the jockeys try to block their enemies' horses, and the runner-up waits for the most propitious moment before entering the *canapi*. In fact, this literal jockeying for position can go on for so long that the sun actually sets and the entire race must be postponed to the next afternoon—much to the shock and chagrin of those tourists who have a flight home the next morning. (You should always allow a few extra days when coming to see the Palio.)

After the final trial the evening before the race, the *contradaioli* gather for a banquet. For this mammoth dinner every public square, every street, every garden is lit up and filled with tables. Thousands of *contradaioli* and their guests eat an open-air meal in a atmosphere thick with expectation and excitement. These are beautiful nights; the magical aura of Siena can give a visitor the impression that time has stopped.

It's a tradition that first the prior, then the captain, and finally the jockey makes a speech promising a battle, thus raising the hopes of the members and triggering endless rounds of toasting, singing, and prayers for victory. The meal usually continues deep into the night, with rivers of red wine that only stop flowing when the last *contradaiolo* finally totters home to bed, completely knackered.

On these occasions the jockeys become king for a night, envied by men and sought out by women, who feel no shame in seducing them. For the more inexperienced among them, this unexpected attention can be dangerous; fortunately a few *contradaioli* are assigned to accompany each of them to bed, almost like bodyguards, to ensure that they be ready and in perfect shape for the next day. In the meantime the horse remains quietly ensconced in its stable, where the *barbaresco* sits up all night, watching over the animal's sleep.

The morning of the big day arrives. In the main church the bishop celebrates a mass for the jockeys, and after the last trial—called the *provaccia*—the jockeys are registered in the town hall. In each *contrada* chapel the traditional blessing of the horse takes place to a capacity crowd. The priest concludes by breaking the silence of the solemn event by virtually shouting at the horse and jockey, *"Go forth, and come back victorious!"*

Then begins the procession, in which members of each *contrada*, dressed in splendid medieval livery, depart the cathedral and parade through the streets of the city to the Campo. Once inside the square, the procession, with its vibrant colors and waving banners, is led by a several contingents from the town hall: six armed soldiers, the communal band, the representatives of the people carrying the flags of every commune of the ancient Republic of Siena, the representatives of the guilds and the Sienese University, and finally representatives of Massa Marittima and Montalcino (communes that have played an important part in Sienese history). Then follow the *contrade*, each represented by two pages, two flagmen, and a drummer; the jockey, riding a horse pulled by a groom; the captain; and finally the racehorse, led by the *barbaresco*. During the entirety of the procession, the flagmen exhibit their skill by launching their standards into the air in a dazzling display of choreographed athleticism. These flagmen are audience favorites, and their virtuoso performances are the result of year-round training. The best of them is rewarded at the end of the procession with the Masgalano.

The procession concludes with a cart—called the *carroccio*—pulled by four oxen and followed by knights who represent the ancient noble families of Siena. On the *carroccio* is mounted the black-and-white flag of Siena, and the Palio itself—the painted banner that is the much-longed-for prize for the winning district. The *contradaioli*, territorially arranged in homogeneous clumps inside the square, greet the entrance of "the cloth" by waving the scarves of their *contrade* (by far the most ubiquitous fashion item of the day).

After one final, collective flag toss, the Palio is hoisted to the corner of the square next to the box where the captains are seated. At the explosion of the cracker, the horses exit the town hall. Each jockey seizes the *nerbo* (whip) handed to him by a representative of the Commune of Siena and sets off toward the starting line. As the jockeys proceed slowly toward the ropes, the tension is indescribable; no one, not even the jockeys themselves, knows the order in which they will align. This is just being decided by a special mechanical device.

At this point it's not unusual to see the jockeys talk furtively among themselves, trying to make some last-minute deals. When the order of alignment has been finalized, the *mossiere* reads it aloud and the jockeys, one by one, approach the final *canapo*. Obviously, the first positions are the best; roars of joy erupt from the *contradaioli* whose horses are called to enter before the others.

It's a difficult task to get the horses aligned in the right order, especially with the jockeys doing anything they can to gain space. The starter must have nerves of steel, because the anxiety of the crowd begins to boil over with each agonizing minute of shuffling and reshuffling. Once the first nine horses are aligned, it only remains for the tenth to decide the start; the moment this animal enters, the ropes will come down. The runner-up position is considered the worst, even though this jockey is able to influence the first few moments of the race considerably, favoring a friendly *contrada* (by entering when it's in a good position) or hampering an enemy (by entering when its horse isn't properly aligned).

The race itself is over in less than two minutes. During those ninety-plus seconds in which the winning horse completes three turns around the square, anything can happen. Jockeys whip each other, trying to unseat their rivals. Some horses, while taking the more dangerous curves, crash against the mattresses and throw their bareback jockeys onto the track, then continue running wildly. It's sheer pandemonium, but it's not crucial to the outcome: The horse that first crosses the finish line wins—with or without its jockey on its back.

For those ninety seconds of the race, the crowd in the Campo is in a state of euphoric hypersensitivity; time seems suspended as every second of the race is recorded by thousands and thousands of eyes. For days afterward every detail will be analyzed and reanalyzed and debated and redebated.

But first there is the rush of victory. The winning horse is swarmed by the victorious *contradaioli*, who leap the barricades to embrace it, even kiss it on the mouth. The victorious jockey is carried away, as is the Palio itself. Thus begins a seemingly endless period of celebration, with dinner after dinner after dinner, countless toasts and choruses of the anthems, and parades around the streets in which the Palio is carried in triumph and shown with pride to the whole city. For weeks the territory of the victorious *contrada* will remain illuminated, and only after months of festivities will the celebrations be concluded with a victory dinner at which the horse, in recognition of its importance, will eat at the head of the table.

No matter how much I try, it's impossible to convey the full significance a victory has for the Sienese citizens in their daily lives. To understand, you must simply have been born in Siena and have lived the life of the *contrada*. For the Palio isn't just a horse race run on the second of July and the sixteenth of August, even if on those dates the emotions are the strongest and the consequences the greatest; no, the Palio is merely the most visible evidence of the associations and traditions that set the pace and tone of Sienese life, and that demand year-round participation. Even as a member of the Noble *Contrada* of the Caterpillar, I am astonished at the enormous time the *contrada* devotes to organizing assemblies, dinners, feasts, competitions, and activities for children and the elderly. In summer the production skills required to celebrate a victory include imagination, enthusiasm, hard labor, and strong economic investment.

The only way to begin to understand the Palio is to take part in the event personally, coming to Siena a few days before the race and living the life of the city as its excitement builds to delirium. I always endeavor to integrate my clients into as much of the preparatory phases as possible—taking them to the drawing of the horses, the trials, the dinners—to give them an idea of the excitement and to help them feel the tension that precedes the event. Usually they remain so impressed and moved that they return again. And again. And again.

To that Texas millionaire who phoned me in the middle of the night, convinced that all this could be purchased as a birthday present for his wife, I merely replied, "I'm sorry, organizing Palios isn't my line. Try another agency." I politely excused myself from helping him figure out which agency that might be, and went back to sleep.

And I dreamed that the Caterpillar won the next Palio.

US VERSUS THEM

I've spent some of the previous chapters discussing various rivalries. I can imagine that a foreigner might find it hard to understand the web of regional animosities that envelops this country, especially if you have the impression that Italy has been a single nation for thousands of years. In fact, Italy was unified only in 1860, by Garibaldi, our first national hero, who couldn't have been more prophetic when he said, "Well, I have made Italy, now someone must make the Italians." No one has yet succeeded. Mussolini came close, instilling in us a powerful sense of unity for nigh on twenty years, but after his inglorious end, this feeling dissolved like sugar in water.

For a small country Italy comprises many wildly different geographies and climates, and these of course contribute to the vast differences among many of our people at different points on the compass. Randomly pick an inhabitant of each of the two extremes of Italy, and you may well find that the one from the north is blond with clear eyes, eats sausages with krauts, drinks beer and grappa, speaks German, lives in mountains submerged by snow six months of the year, and answers to a name like Kurt, Gustav, Norbert, or Gerda. Meanwhile his countryman from the southernmost tip will not astonish by being shorter, with a darker complexion and a big black mustache (even on some of the women!), a diet of bread, figs, red wine, and *limoncello*, and a name like Salvatore, Concetta, or Assunta Maria—and, in general, a stronger cultural affinity for the nearby North African states than for Italy's Nordic neighbors. How can such varied individuals possibly be united under the same flag when they don't even speak the same language?

It's generally agreed that the major cultural division in Italy is between north and south. The problem is establishing the border between the two. For a resident of Trentino, the south begins in Milan; for a Milanese, in Bologna; for a Bolognese, in Florence; for a Florentine, in Rome—and so on. In Tuscany we consider ourselves neither; we don't want to be considered part of the rather drowsy south, nor do we desire affiliation with the often superficial north. It appeals to us to be considered simply Tuscans.

Or perhaps not so simply. In previous centuries Tuscany itself was divided into many small city-states, each with its own independent government. For this reason each city remains vividly distinct from the others, with noticeable differences in everything from architecture to dialect. And as I have often noted, the memories of ancient wars, feuds, and rivalries among these city-states remain very much alive. The Florentines, for example, are disdained by all other Tuscans, who consider them vulgar, arrogant, and pompous. The Florentines, in turn, mock the Sienese with an insulting rhyme: *"Siena di tre cose è piena: torri, campane, e figli di puttane"*—"Siena of three things is full: towers, bells, and sons of whores."

In Siena we never tire of reminding the Florentines of their humiliating defeat in the battle of Montaperti in 1260. If Siena faces Florence in any sporting match, you can be sure that someone in the crowd will unfurl a banner boasting REMEMBER MON-TAPERTI! to raise the ire of the Florentine spectators. For their response they can turn to Dante, a Florentine who in his *Divina Commedia* depicted the Sienese as the most vain of all peoples, and refers to our victory as having "dyed the Arbia red with blood."

(One irony not lost on the Sienese and other Tuscans is that, in our travels, it is sometimes more convenient to say we are from Florence. It's easier than naming Siena, or Prato, or Pistoia—or, in my case, Castellina in Chianti. Almost anywhere in the world, from California to Capetown, these names elicit nothing but dull stares. So we say "Florence" just to see a spark of light in our interlocutor's eyes.)

The roll call of rivalries continues with Siena and Arezzo. Here the *aretini* suffer still from a nasty inferiority complex resulting from the lesser splendor and influence of their city in the Middle Ages. The Sienese, for their part, call the *aretini* "toads" and look down on the mass immigration of *aretino* peasants to the Republic of Siena in search of a better life.

The list goes on seemingly endlessly: Pistoia against her neighbors Lucca and Prato, Grosseto against Siena and Livorno, Massa against Carrara, and so on. The only unanimous alliance between the cities is the one against Pisa; in fact, the expression *"Meglio un morto in casa che un pisano all'uscio"* ("Better a dead man in your house than a *pisano* on your doorstep") is idiomatic in whatever city of Tuscany you visit.

I've covered the more important cities, but also worth consideration is the presence in every single province of many rivalries among its villages. In the Sienese area there are frequent fistfights between loyalists of Poggibonsi and those of Colle Val d'Elsa, two localities just about 5 miles apart. I can recall a heated discussion between a distinguished lawyer of Montepulciano and an equally respected doctor of Montalcino, each ready to come to blows to defend the honor of his town against the other.

Soccer games between towns bring out the worst of these kinds of behavior. I've seen calm, imperturbable family men transform suddenly into hooligans, returning quietly to normal at the end of the game. I've witnessed elegant, Prada-wearing ladies express their disapproval with a rival town's referee in bellowed phrases I blushingly decline to translate. I've seen grandfathers teach their own grandsons obscenities to shout at the opposing team.

And of course it doesn't stop at intervillage conflicts. As among the *contrade* of Siena, rivalries also exist inside each city, with no lessening of ardor and intensity. Possibly the disposition for rivalry extends even more deeply into Italian society than this—among neighbors, among family members . . . Still, I think we must consider, at such a point, that it becomes none of our business.

AUGUST AND THE LOVERS

Now the heat sizzles, but at these altitudes the nights are always cool and delightful. I recline in the shade, the quiet broken only by the eerie whir of the cicadas. Often in these periods forest fires can flare up, terrifying to observe yet undeniably exciting—the thrill is visceral and primal when pines burst suddenly into flames like kitchen matches.

The wildflowers are still abundant; in late summer they reach their apex and stand tall and stately, swaying dispassionately in the wind. But dominating the fields is wild fennel, with its tiny yellow flowers and its feathered dark green leaves, oozing the unmistakable aromas of aniseed and licorice into the torrid summer air.

In Italy, in August, everything comes to a halt—the schools, the offices, the stores, the large industries of the north, even the Parliament. The cities empty of their inhabitants, who, in search of tranquillity and pure air, move en masse toward the coasts, taking with them all the chaos and pollution from which they're trying to escape. Likewise, in Chianti life slows to a crawl. Farmers don't have much to do in the vineyards, most of the arduous task of cultivation having already been attended to, while the grape harvest is yet two months away. All that remains is for the grapes to ripen; this is literally their time in the sun.

On one typically torpid August morning, I woke up very early. Outside the window it was still predawn; everything was preternaturally still, without even a hint of a breeze. In the limpid sky the last stars were slowly melting behind the hills, and a sudden red flare announced the coming sunrise.

I could immediately feel that the air was warmer than usual, and in fact during breakfast Cristina said she'd heard on television that the day's temperatures would be record breaking. Given the propensity of newscasters to be alarmists, I didn't give this too much thought and donned my usual work "uniform": long-sleeved white shirt worn outside my blue jeans and a pair of heavy winter boots. I kissed Cristina good-bye, opened the sunroof in the van, and left for Florence, where a couple on honeymoon were waiting for me.

As you have now doubt learned by now, I am never very enthusiastic about having to go all the way to Florence to pick up customers, but in August the empty roads make the trip almost enjoyable, and it's a kind of surreal pleasure to drive the city streets alone, as though they were reserved for my private use. Everywhere I look, storefronts are shuttered, the ubiquitous orange CHIUSO PER FERIE (CLOSED FOR VACATION) signs hung on the doors. The only people in town are the tourists, who seem to enjoy strolling through a Florence without traffic, without smog, and above all without Florentines (a very great advantage). The main problem is surviving in the oppressive heat that can, due to the city's unfortunate situation at the bottom of a valley surrounded by mountains, reach African proportions.

I parked right in front of the hotel—again, something possible only in this off-kilter month—and tried to enter the hotel, but my way was blocked by a young couple seated on the steps before the entrance kissing each other passionately. I was a little shy of interrupting such ravishment, so I waited a few minutes, thinking it would either run its course—quite the opposite, it become more energetic—or that they would become aware of my presence, though if they did, it didn't in any way inhibit them. Finally I decided to squeeze around them. By pressing my back against the railing and emptying the air out of my lungs, I was just able to shimmy behind the lovers' shoulders.

At the reception desk the concierge, sweltering within his starched, penguin-style suit, politely asked if I needed any help. "I have an appointment with Mr. and Mrs. Perez," I said.

"The lady and the gentlemen," he replied, his professional tone never faltering, "are waiting for you outside."

I could have slapped my hand against my forehead. Why hadn't it occurred to me that the couple manhandling each other on the stairs were my honeymooners? I went back through the enormous wooden door and found them still engaged in the same activity. This time I didn't bother being subtle, but barked out "Mr. and Mrs. Perez?" They immediately pulled apart, leapt to their feet, and busily smoothed their hair and clothes, like soldiers caught sleeping during a night vigil.

We made our introductions. They immediately struck me as a beautiful couple: little more than twenty-five years old, both Cuban Americans born in Florida and natives of Miami, where they managed a successful shoe business. All these preliminaries were exchanged on our way to the van. Once we reached it, conversation ceased; they crawled into the backseat, and before I could even turn the ignition key, they had recommenced necking with abandon.

Very embarrassed, I decided to take refuge in feigned obliviousness. I began reciting my usual historical and cultural spiel, but they obviously weren't hearing a word I said. I regretted not having installed one of those electric dividing screens that come standard in limousines.

I pulled into our first port of call. *Now they'll stop*, I thought—rather too optimistically, as it turned out. Not even walking the open streets of a small, picturesque Tuscan village was sufficient distraction from each other's charms. In front of the church, they kissed; every two steps a kiss; inside the bar they kissed so much that the coffee they ordered grew cold and undrinkable. Once we got back into the car and they disappeared beneath the range of my rearview mirror, I stopped speaking altogether. I put in a cassette of romantic music and began wandering around the countryside, forgetting the itinerary. And all the while the temperature climbed higher and higher.

The situation was getting more than a little awkward; how could I endure a whole day with two such customers? I had to either come up with a solution or face the fact that I'd become a glorified chauffeur. (With perhaps a hint of pimp!) Then suddenly a stroke of genius: the *tombolotti*! Why hadn't I thought of it before?

The *tombolotti* is one of those places so beautiful and uncontaminated that you feel the conflicting urges to tell everyone you know about it, and to keep it entirely to yourself. This time I had no trouble deciding. After following an endless, winding road, I parked at the top of a hill, beneath the shade of a mulberry tree. I said, "Okay, guys, a slight change in the program." Their addled heads reappeared in my rearview mirror; they'd been so enraptured by each other that they hadn't even realized I'd stopped the car.

I gave them a moment to collect themselves, then opened the door to let them out. "I'm going to conduct you to a romantic, isolated spot," I explained while the young lovers followed me with piqued curiosity. We descended a steep path that led to the bottom of a valley bordered by Sangiovese vines, the sun beating ferociously on our shoulders all the while. Here the soil was so rocky that it seemed impossible anything could grow in it; nevertheless, in October, in this very field, would be harvested one of the finest grapes in Chianti. It's one of the area's miraculous little paradoxes.

At the end of the path, we made our way through a brush of Spanish broom and multicolored wildflowers and into a forest of oak and acacia, where small, sudden movements coming from the bushes made my clients jump. To put them at their ease, I told them that these were probably made by the ubiquitous lizards—though I wonder now if a warning about the lethal Tuscan viper might not have been just the thing to put the chill on my clients' romantic ardor.

At the opposite end of the small forest, we emerged at our destination. The sweat-streaked faces of the young lovers, which during the long descent had been knotted with perplexity, now lit up with smiles of astonishment. They found themselves in a small clearing. A little stream sluiced through a cove of thick green vegetation, in places digging out of the rocky banks a series of natural bathtubs filled with water so transparent that river crabs can be seen scuttling along the bottom—an incontestable sign of purity. The brook flows through this clearing with enough force to form a series of small waterfalls and receiving pools, all connected. A screen of vegetation encircles each pool, as though nature deliberately and jealously wishes to hide it.

I said, "If you like, you can stay here all day." They seemed very happy with the idea, so I added, "Fine, it's all yours. I'll return in a few hours with something to eat. If you like, you can bathe completely naked; I guarantee you no one will come down here. When I return I'll call from the top of the valley to give you a warning that I'm coming down."

The newlyweds seemed thrilled; they'd found a small corner of paradise, and what's more, they had it all to themselves. Visibly moved, they thanked me and started kissing again. I stayed long enough to give them a few recommendations; as I did so I observed the surface of the water, on which skated many small insects, and I smiled to note that their shadows, reflected on the bottom of the pool, oddly resembled the marks left by cats' paws on car hoods.

During my slow return to the top of the hill, I passed through a storm of amorous butterflies and was amused and intrigued by the fact that each one seemed to chase a partner that was similarly colored—as though it were a sort of team game. The most audacious ones rested on my sweat-slick arms, giving me a hardly perceptible tickle. Dragonflies of different but invariably immense dimensions traced invisible geometric lines in the air, at the same time mating with such robust precision as to cast a pall over even the most audacious practitioners of the Kama Sutra.

The *tombolotti* had been a discovery of my teenage years, when I wandered wildly through the forests in search of the maximum isolation from daily life. It was in those kinds of places that I began to investigate and appreciate the psychedelic world, smoking my first joints and listening to the kind of music that transports your mind to a different level, making you feel like an integral part of the surrounding environment.

I waited a few hours, then returned with fruit, bottled water, and sandwiches filled with Oriano's best homemade salami and ham. I found the young lovers under one of the ice-cold waterfalls that fall from the cliff, still entwined in each other's arms.

We ate the sandwiches seated on a smooth expanse of rock, amusing ourselves by feeding the fish with bread crumbs, or holding our legs still in the water until they were bold enough to approach and nibble at our calves with extreme delicacy. From the numbers of fish our skin attracted, I can only presume it must be a delicacy in the aquatic world.

After lunch I left the couple alone once more, and late in the evening I returned to pick them up. When I announced that it was time to return to Florence, they were so disappointed that they looked even more youthful—like children suddenly deprived of a favorite game. On the road back I inserted a cassette of love songs, turned the rearview mirror aside to give them privacy, and without saying a word let them kiss the whole way.

Nine months later they phoned to thank me for that memorable day in the wilds of Chianti and to announce that now they were three: They had had a beautiful baby boy. They named him Dario.

INTERVALLO

The American Caterpillar

Certain people, when they depart this world, leave behind an almost tangible legacy, something more than mere spirit, a permanent furrow in a uncultivated field. One such person was Roy Moskovitz, the American of the Caterpillar, a man who not only broke down the clannish walls of Sienese society and *contrada* exclusivity but also made himself so indelibly a part of both that his closest friends here still speak of him in the present tense.

After having written many pages about people I've met personally, I feel a bit awkward dedicating a chapter to someone I never actually encountered. Yet a book about Americans in Tuscany would be incomplete without him; he was one of the few foreigners in anyone's recollection who came to understand deeply the significance of our city, and the exact nature of "Sienesity." One of his favorite aphorisms was "No one is born Sienese. One becomes Sienese." An arguable sentiment, certainly—except that he himself proved it, living in our city for many years, learning and embracing all its deepest values, and finding acceptance among its people, who adopted him like a son. He knew our history and cultural achievements better almost than we did; he interpreted and praised the spirit of *contrada* aggregation; in short, he reflected back at us an image of ourselves that we would not have seen without him, and in this way carved for himself an important space in daily Sienese life.

But who was he really—this distinguished Jewish gentleman, baby faced and pear shaped and always fitted out with a neat bow tie? As a matter of fact, we don't know very much about him. He was rather reserved when talking about his private life, and unfortunately our curiosity about him was never a match for his about us. We do know he was a professor of literature who adored classical music; that he lived in New York City; and that apparently the Noble *Contrada* of the Bruco was as close to a family as he ever had, so much so that on his death he bequeathed us a large part of his estate and many personal effects.

On a certain summer evening, during one of our daily dinners, seated at the table in the splendid Bruco gardens, I asked a group of *contradaioli* who had known Roy whether they knew the exact spelling of his surname, as I had decided to mention him in the chapter of this book dedicated to the Palio. Their faces lit up at the mention of his name, and many started speaking at once—giving me much more than the spelling of *Moskovitz*. Which is how Roy has come to have his own chapter. For the remainder of that dinner—during which he was often toasted—and later, examining the newspaper archives, I learned the following about Roy Moskovitz.

Like many tourists, he arrived in Siena to experience the Palio. As he passed through the Porta Ovile and climbed the steep Via del Comune, he noticed a large throng in front of the chapel of the Caterpillar. He asked what was going on and was told that the horse was being blessed for the race. Why the blessing of a horse took on such an epochal role in Roy's life is a mystery (though it was the mid-1960s, when everything was a bit topsy-turvy); all he knew was that, as he later put it, "The bell of my destiny had chimed." He entered the church, lost himself among the hundreds of people crammed in the nave, and experienced such strong emotion that after the service he felt compelled to follow the Palio in the Campo, among the people of the Bruco. The Caterpillar didn't win the race that day, but it won something more enduring—the complete adoration of Roy Moskovitz. He decided to remain in town for the ensuing month and follow also the August Palio.

This time he purchased a ticket for the bleachers; he also made a down payment on the hearts of his chosen *contrada*, and such were his enthusiasm, curiosity, and exquisite courtesy that he was accepted by them in record time. He was baptized a member in 1972, during a ceremony in which he was quite visibly moved; and onlookers were so awed by his emotion that they felt no urge to giggle at the sight of this grown man sharing the baptismal font with a cluster of wailing infants.

In no time the "Professore" became "Signor Moskovitz" and later, to his joy, simply Roy. He began peppering his conversations with references to "We Sienese"—made the more charming by his distinctive, if pleasant, American accent. He rented a room in town, and whenever possible would leap a plane and fly to us. He spent summers among us, only returning to the States in September, when he left (always reluctantly) to resume his teaching duties. When he retired he expanded his time in Siena to nine months a year, so that, inevitably, a friend greeted him one day by exclaiming, "Welcome back home! How was your vacation in America?"

During all this time Roy steadily accumulated his vast

knowledge of our city, an uncanny storehouse he wielded gently but devastatingly. It wasn't unusual for him, during his daily walks, to call his companions to a halt before some minor statue, painting, or shrine, then offer a detailed lecture on the work's origin and history—a fascinating but often humbling experience for his listeners, who may have spent their lives blithely passing the object in question.

His knowledge extended beyond the city walls to the surrounding countryside. Not a single church escaped his relentless curiosity, even those tucked away in the remotest corners of the province, and it wasn't uncommon for the local priests to come and greet him warmly on his arrival.

His friendships with the clergy weren't limited to country parsons, though. Once, he was scandalized by a painting in the Duomo. It was a mere copy, he insisted. His companions were dubious: "Roy, what are you talking about? This is the *Duomo*." He insisted on seeing the bishop, who, it turned out, was an old acquaintance who greeted him with open arms. "You're right, Roy," the bishop said to Roy's accusation, "the work is a copy, put up for preservation purposes. No one's ever noticed till now. Come with me, I'll show you the original." He then led Roy and his speechless friends to an interior office where he opened a safe, revealing the genuine painting. Roy spent several minutes in silent contemplation of it, then exclaimed, "All right, now I'm happy, we can go."

It wasn't unusual to encounter him walking the city streets alone in the middle of the night, idly seeking some small curiosity that had thus far escaped his notice, or perhaps simply taking in the atmosphere of the picturesque alleyways. Fortunately much of Roy's knowledge remains accessible to us, because he wrote often for the Caterpillar's magazine about the art and culture of Siena.

Roy maintained a tremendous respect for everyone, and was never heard to speak a bad word about anyone. He was rather witty, though his Anglo-Saxon sense of humor wasn't always understood. He also dressed in a donnish manner quite strange to Italian eyes: scruffy but unmistakably gentlemanly, with an aura of intellectual eccentricity. A man of surprisingly simple tastes, all he required for perfect happiness was good company, a glass of red wine, and a cigar. Even when, at Palio time, it seemed the cards were stacked against the Caterpillar, he was never demoralized; it seemed to him to be a minor detail. To him the *contrada* was heaven itself, and no prize banner could conceivably improve it. Still, he loved listening to the inevitable and heated discussions about the race. He often said, with as much admiration as amusement, that whenever two Sienese talk about the Palio there are always three opinions.

Roy's arrival was always an excuse for a feast, and it began to seem that his returns to the States were a form of rest cure for him, necessary to cleanse and detox after all the three-hour meals and liters of wine he consumed daily. At every return he would remark that the streets of Siena got steeper and the bleachers for the Palio tighter. The women of the Caterpillar told me that often he would come to our headquarters with stains on his shirts and jackets so tight he could no longer button them up.

A friend, Mario, remembered the day Roy accompanied him to Florence. They stopped for breakfast in an elegant cafe in one of the city's larger squares, and as soon as they entered, all the waiters rushed up to greet him—"Signor Roy, Signor Roy!" They immediately laid the best table in the house, and Mario sat by, dumbstruck, when in place of the traditional cappuccino and roll, aromatic sausages and bacon began appearing unbidden at the table.

Once it happened that some Caterpillars surprised Roy on his home ground. Arriving in New York on business, they phoned him from the airport; he was delighted, and immediately invited them to come and visit him in Manhattan. "I live on West Seventy-seventh Street near Central Park," he said. Fine, his friends said; but at what number? "That's a minor detail," he said dismissively. "When you get here, you'll know." His friends, somewhat perplexed, filed into a cab, and when they reached the Upper West Side, they wondered how they could have been so foolish as to set out without a building number. Imposing apartment buildings loomed impersonally over them on all sides. Finally they turned onto Seventy-seventh Street and were stunned to see, flapping gloriously from an upper window of a very tall building, an enormous Caterpillar flag, its intense yellow, blue, and green reflecting brilliantly the noonday sky.

Roy had by no means abandoned his own country in favor of Italy; he was a true American (born on the Fourth of July), and for his birthday always gave a dinner with lots of little American and Caterpillar flags decorating the table. And this odd habit—feting himself on his own birthday—brings to mind another of his sterling qualities: his generosity. It was impossible to offer him a drink or a meal; he always insisted on paying for everyone present. He even set up a scholarship for the students of the *contrada*, named after his niece Sylvia.

Eventually Roy received a special commendation from the mayor. That day, on some pretext or other, some friends brought him to the town hall; he was shocked to find the city council in session, along with many people he knew, all elegantly dressed. When he realized the gathering was in his honor, tears of emotion streamed down his face.

A dear friend of his wrote, "He seemed to have friends

everywhere . . . in England, Ireland, Holland, Scandinavia, Vienna, and in his beloved Italy, especially in Siena. When I came to visit him there in 1990, we got out of a taxi together, and before we could even cross the street, a small swarm of people came forward to greet him and embrace him. He exchanged a few words with them and they departed happily; he then turned to me and said, shrugging his shoulders, 'I have no idea who they are.' This happened several times afterward; people everywhere sought him out—they called him *Professore Roy*."

One of Roy's other defining characteristics was his inability to pass by a good restaurant or say no to a good glass of wine, despite the years taking their toll on him and his body growing heavier. He would admit that his doctors had repeatedly ordered him to stop eating and drinking so much and look after himself, but he simply couldn't renounce the pleasures of life. Then he'd add, darkly but with a smile, that a number of the doctors who had prescribed these rigorous diets were now dead anyway.

During Palio season he always wore a rosette with our colors. He lived the event intensely, but alas, he was never able to experience a Caterpillar victory. Eventually he did in fact become ill, and his disease took progressively greater hold of him until he was no longer able to return to his beloved Siena. A very close friend of his, Pier Guido, whom I visited in his stamp shop on the main street of Siena, told me that during his last years he would phone Roy while watching the race on television and give him running commentary. He said that when in August 1996 the Caterpillar finally, after forty-one endless years, triumphed with a splendid victory, Roy was in extreme pain due to his disease; all the same he had to put down the receiver, as the emotion was too strong for his heart.

A few days later Roy called back saying that his phone had

been ringing constantly for days, so many people from Siena had phoned to give him the news. His voice trembled as he said this; he hadn't realized so many people thought so well of him.

Every month, on the anniversary of the victory, Pier Guido sent Roy a postcard with an image of the costumes worn by the Caterpillar in the pageants. While telling me this, he opened a drawer and produced the remainder of the stack of postcards he'd purchased for this purpose, never sent; for Roy died in 1997 at the age of ninety. The people who visited him in his last days were struck by how popular he'd become among the hospital personnel.

Pier Guido now keeps the postcards as a kind of relic. "In memory of Roy," he added fondly, "I have from that day always followed the Palio on TV."

When news of his death reached Siena, innumerable newspaper articles paid tribute to him, and placards were posted all over the city announcing his passing. In the Caterpillar someone even composed verses in his honor.

Maybe one day the story of Roy will become urban folklore, passed orally from generation to generation, till future Sienese refer to the old American gentleman who, sick in bed in New York, heard that his *contrada* had won the Palio and died with a smile on his face. This isn't what really happened, of course, but in its simplification of Roy's story, it reaches perhaps a purer truth. I can't help thinking Roy would enjoy the tribute himself. The important thing for him would be to become part of Siena's history, whether as history, legend . . . or fairy tale.

PLAYING OFFENSE

Returning to rivalries, I want to mention an episode a pair of unprepared clients of mine had the misfortune of experiencing. I spent the day in question with two friendly young American couples, and during lunch we somehow found ourselves discussing basketball. The two men were quite keen on the subject, and we passed the remainder of the meal comparing notes on memorable games, the names of key players, and so on, much to the chagrin of the two wives. As it happened, that very evening the Siena team was appearing in an important play-off game against Bologna. I proposed to my customers that they accompany me to see what the game is like over here.

The women politely declined, then turned and said with a laugh, "We didn't come all the way to Italy to go to a basketball game!"—obviously hoping to elicit some kind of corroboration from their husbands. But the effort was in vain; the spark of the sports fanatic had been ignited in the men's eyes, and after a brief, perfunctory verbal tussle, the wives gave up and released their husbands into my care. I confess I felt a little guilty.

In most of Italy soccer is the most popular sport, drawing the largest crowds, the biggest sponsors, and the most lucrative contracts. Siena, however, is a small city without the resources to build a nationally competitive soccer team. Our public institutions and sponsors have thus turned instead to basketball, forging a team that can, and has, taken its place at the highest level of the Italian professional league.

The Italian championship is considered among the most competitive in the world, so much so that for many young American players it represents a springboard to the NBA—or, at the opposite end, an honorable way for former NBA players to finish their careers. And Italian fans are if anything more fervent than their American counterparts. In Siena the *Mens Sana Basket* is nearly a religion, followed by people of all ages and sponsored by the local bank.

That evening, as we parked outside the stadium, Brian and Paul—my clients—were immediately struck by two things: the incredible noise coming from within and the sight of policemen in riot gear escorting five busloads of Bolognese fans through the gates. At the entrance we were searched for concealed weapons; we then made our way to our seats. As soon as we sat down, I pointed out the section reserved for the visiting team—a virtual cage, surrounded by metal bars. It was also still empty. I explained that the policemen would only allow the Bolognese to enter a few minutes before the game began.

The arena was designed to hold approximately 6,000 spectators; at the start of the game, it was practically bulging with frenzied fans. Among them were Sienese teenagers who had prepared a series of beautifully choreographed set pieces involving colored smoke, banners, and offensive slogans to chant at the Bolognese.

Brian and Paul were somewhat stunned by all the confusion, and even more so by seeing two old NBA greats, Dominic Wilkins and Doc Rivers, now playing for Bologna. While the loudspeaker announced the entrance on the court of the Sienese players, the Bologna fans interrupted with a deafening din of drums and trumpets, then turned their backs toward us, dropped their pants, and mooned us.

Brian and Paul were initially amused by this. They only became aware of the full gravity of these insults when the Sienese fans swarmed the visitors' cage, shrieking in rage and launching obscenities (and spittle) over the cage walls.

The game began. Each time the referee penalized Siena, objects of all kinds were hurled angrily onto the court. My guests could not believe their eyes. They were accustomed to the highly civilized behavior of American fans, who calmly enjoy the game while munching on popcorn, leaving their seats only to visit the restroom or the concession stand, certainly never to propel themselves toward the court in a howling, murderous fury. These Italian fans must have looked to them like utter savages. When, at the next controversial decision, the game was temporarily halted because of an invasion of the court by several hotheads, Brian and Paul were deeply shocked. Fortunately they didn't understand a single word of Italian, so at least the foul epithets and offensive songs had no more effect on them than background noise.

They were fascinated not so much by the level of play—less spectacular than is the norm for the NBA—as by the ongoing freak show put on by the opposing factions: the continuous drumming, the constant rude chants. The Sienese section was a tumultuous beehive of angry fans in green and white, the Bolognese cage a boiling kettle of sociopaths in black and white. I tried to explain to my guests that in Italy people are interested exclusively in the result of the game, and that this often ruins any chance of fancy play—unlike the United States, where a single player's consummate skill and grace can exalt his team's fans even in the event of a defeat.

The game was admittedly exciting and very close. At three seconds from the buzzer, Siena was ahead by two points and had possession of the ball; victory seemed secure. Instead, an incredible Hail Mary shot gave the victory to Bologna in the very last second. The Sienese, who had been on their feet confidently singing the "Verbena"—one of the city's anthems—suddenly fell deadly quiet, while the Bolognese exploded in a roar of joy and started taunting the home fans about this last-second disgrace.

And then all hell broke loose. A group of Sienese leapt onto the court and started chasing the poor referee, accusing him of having validated the last shot after the buzzer sounded. Another group of berserk fans stormed after the retreating Bologna team, forcing them to barricade themselves in the locker room.

The bedlam continued with a furious hail of coins, of which poor Brian was a victim; he was hit square in the forehead with a hundred-*lire* missile, with sufficient force to require that I take him to first aid for treatment. As we made our way through the uproar, the Bologna supporters again mooned the locals, triggering such a surge of fury that the Sienese at last overcame the riot police and swarmed into the cage. The Bolognese had not had time to get their pants back up, and the Sienese took advantage of this by tearing them off completely and carrying them outside the stadium, then pausing long enough to smash the bus windows. The Bolognese were thus forced to ride home half naked, amid shattered glass, with the cold wind whipping between their bare legs.

After leaving the first aid office, with Brian holding a bag of ice over his swollen forehead, we returned to our seats to collect

Paul, but there was no sign of him. We searched the stadium with growing panic until a policeman asked us if we needed help; I told him we'd lost an American tourist. He asked me if by any chance he was wearing a black-and-white jacket. I nodded. The policeman pointed out a station close by and said, "Your friend's been hurt; they're medicating him in there."

I raced to the station, followed by Brian, who hadn't understood what the policeman said and was still a bit stunned by his own injury. Inside, we found Paul in the hands of a doctor who was stitching up his cheek.

"What happened to *you*?" Brian asked.

"I'm not sure," he said dazedly. "I only know that at some point someone punched me in the face and ran off." Reconstructing the incident in my head, I realized that Paul had been mistaken for a Bolognese fan because of the colors of his jacket and was consequently attacked by a crazed local.

The Bologna section was by now deserted and looked like an abandoned battlefield: Everywhere were strewn banners, clothes, bags, other objects, and debris. Soon the entire arena, which only half an hour before had echoed with the beating of drums and the clamor of voices, was empty. The only spectators left were Brian and me, as we waited for the stitching of Paul's face to be completed.

I was mortified. All day I'd been boasting that Siena was a quiet city with no crime, a safe place where violence never rears its ugly head. Now I'd led two of the very people I'd been boasting to into a kind of human maelstrom, and they'd both emerged much the worse for wear.

As I drove them back to the hotel, the initial fright passed, and they even began to see the funny side of it. On their return to the States, they'd sure as hell have something different to tell their friends! Unfortunately, their wives were considerably less amused. The shock of seeing their men return to them patched and sewn together set them off; they were going to sue the fans, the team, the police, the city—even me, for having insisted on taking them to the game. I don't remember what I said to them, but somehow I managed to calm them down.

The next morning, after the two couples had flown home, I picked up the local newspaper. The main headline was TWO FANS ATTACKED IN SIENA. I considered sending copies to them as mementos . . . then thought better of it and just bought one for myself.

SEPTEMBER AND THE TIMEKEEPER

All the seasons arrive late in Chianti, and in September there are few signs of autumn. Everywhere the grapes are ripening, and many flowers still bloom—beautiful wild carrots, chicory, and cyclamens, whose pink blossoms open before the leaves appear. The forests grow dense with human fauna as the mushroom hunters swarm across the land in search of delicious porcinis and gentiles. In this season it's best to be on extra guard against the vipers: The females climb the trees to give birth to their young and do not take at all kindly to intrusions.

On a very hot August afternoon—the kind of day on which you sweat even while lying perfectly still—I was reclining in my back garden, reading. The air was particularly humid, and a dense haze had drifted across the valley, hiding the summits of the Abetone, the towers of San Gimignano, and even the nearby hills of the Montagnola Senese. I was drowsy, on the brink of sleep, when the fax machine hummed to life. It was a request from an American lady for my services during the month of September. I answered immediately, sending along a program that seemed ideal for what she had specified: visits to Chianti, Siena, Crete, and Montalcino. It seemed to me an easy three-day affair, from the time I'd pick them up in Florence to the time I'd drop them at the station for their train to Rome.

Voilà—all set! I returned to sweating in my deck chair, once again in the company of my book. Not half an hour had passed before the fax machine again came to life: The lady had agreed, and we were set! *If only it was always so easy to please customers*, I thought contentedly as I jotted the dates into my calendar.

The day arrived, and I drove to a very elegant hotel in Florence to collect my new client and her husband. As always, I had dressed in jeans and white shirt, and as I parked my dusty white van next to the inevitable limousines, I thought I could detect a touch of envy from the drivers in their buttoned-up livery. In front of the hotel, a man was engaged in an argument with one of the drivers. "I never requested your service," he insisted in English, while the driver helplessly waved a sheet of paper at him and replied, "But I have here the reservation from your travel agency in the United States!"

"No," the tourist frostily insisted, "my appointment is with another service." Since I had arrived several minutes early, I passed the time by eavesdropping. The argument rapidly degenerated into a shouting match. The driver wanted to be paid for his services, since at this late hour he could not find another customer for the day, while the American had no intention of giving him a penny.

At one point the tourist said, "I don't need you or your vehicle. I'm waiting for a guide who will take us in his car. His name is Dario and we've had an arrangement with him for more than a month." As soon as I heard my name, I approached and cautiously introduced myself.

"Here you are, then!" the tourist exclaimed, happy that I had arrived to prove his point. The misunderstanding thus appeared to be a simple reservation error, so the driver quickly slipped away, no doubt to try to claim reimbursement from his agency.

My new customer, Mr. Mawson, was a man of about sixty, rather small, and, so it struck me, very nervous—so much so that he seemed to transmit anxiety to those around him. He moved with sudden, short, jerky movements, and kept sneaking quick glances at his watch. I realized that this obsessive attention to the time was a kind of nervous tic, and that it would plague me for the duration of the tour.

A few minutes later his wife arrived. She was a striking woman, elegant and refined, and very different from her husband in that she was quite self-possessed and calm. She, like her husband, was dressed more in keeping with a cocktail party than a country tour, but this was something I was used to by now.

I showed them to the car and began following our mutually agreed-upon itinerary for the first day: a tour of Chianti, ending up in Siena. Immediately Mr. Mawson started bombarding me with questions: "What time will we reach Siena? . . . How long before our first stop? . . . At what precise time will we have lunch? . . ." Always flicking his wrist and checking his watch skittishly. Seeing that he was so preoccupied with the time, I wondered whether he might have some important appointment in Siena or some urgent phone call to make. But when I inquired about this, he said that no, he had no one to see or contact that day.

Despite this, he spent the drive in a state of bone-rattling agitation. He kept looking around with wide, furtive eyes, and every time I braked he, too, pushed his foot against the floorboard as though he were the one driving. After a while I noticed that he was checking his watch even more frequently and sweating profusely. I tried to settle his nerves, reassuring him that in the three days he would spend with me, I would look after everything; he and his wife had only to relax.

At the first stop, at a typical Tuscan hill town, I was halfway through my narration on Chianti's history and culture when he checked his watch again and said, "Very good, very interesting, but it's better if we get moving." I was more than a little taken aback. Evidently the tour wasn't exactly captivating either him or his wife—who, despite having made specific requests for the very sights I was showing her, was visibly ill at ease during the drive along the dusty white roads of Chianti. If I hadn't known better, I'd have thought that every stop on the itinerary was something she was dead set against. Each time I turned off a main thoroughfare onto one of the white stone roads that dip into the forests, she seemed momentarily panicked and looked desperately back, as though she longed to return to the smooth, civilized tarmac.

Each stop provoked the same reaction: Mr. Mawson behaved as though he had a plane to catch, while his wife seemed to be holding her breath till it was all over and she could go shopping.

When we reached Volpaia we went to Gina's place, the only restaurant in town and a place where a menu as such does not exist. Gina, a benign autocrat, serves whatever she has cooked that day, thereby guaranteeing the freshest and most lovingly prepared meals.

That day we were fortunate because she had prepared *ribollita*, a typical Tuscan dish that she cooks with almost divine skill, following a very ancient recipe. She boils cannellini beans and vegetables until they liquefy into a rather dense soup. Into this she dips some slices of bread, then serves it up with a drop of extra-virgin olive oil. Naturally, the *ribollita* was complemented by other traditional Tuscan dishes: *crostini*, homemade ravioli, stewed chicken, rabbit cooked in Chianti, and, to finish off, a splendid *tiramisù*.

My clients didn't eat much; they sat stiffly in their seats with distinctly pained expressions on their faces—in addition to which, of course, Mr. Mawson seemed positively frantic to speed things along. At the end of the meal, he called me aside and said in a low voice, "Dario, I have to give you my honest opinion: If you ever want to get recommendations from your customers, never, ever force them to eat that terrible bean soup. No American will be able to stomach more than a spoonful." I thanked him and pretended to accept his tip gratefully. I didn't bother telling him of the ecstatic reaction Gina's *ribollita* elicited every day from my American customers, or of the number of times I'd had to promise to send the recipe overseas.

Finally the tour concluded. I took the harried pair back to their hotel, which was situated just outside the ancient city walls, not far from my house. We arranged the hour at which we'd meet the next morning for their tour of Siena, and then I bade them good-bye.

Whenever I accompany my clients to Siena, I try to focus on the Palio, both because it's the city's most colorful and accessible event and because it provides a means of understanding the true spirit of the people. Since it's so difficult to describe the deep emotional involvement of the Sienese in this tradition, I usually invite my clients to watch a video filmed during the days that precede and follow the race, in which are visible all the tension, passion, and exuberant renewal that we experience at Palio time. Accordingly, I intended to begin the day at my house, where I would show the Mawsons this video, then take them into Siena itself.

When I picked them up, I outlined this plan for them. Mrs. Mawson immediately objected: "I'd prefer," she said, "to visit the city first and *then* see the video."

Now, Siena is not a frenetic city. The historical center is completely closed to all traffic, even that of bicycles. The only exception to this rule is the early morning, when the shops open and supply vans are permitted to enter the old walls. For these few hours the narrow roads of the ancient city are an angry snarl; it's the very worst time to take a walk there.

I tried to explain this to Mrs. Mawson, pointing out that walking the city would be much more enjoyable after the morning traffic had abated. But she was not to be swayed, and her husband, completely uninterested, kept checking his watch. Today, it turned out, he did indeed have an appointment: He'd decided that in late afternoon he would go for a swim, and for the remainder of the day, that's all he thought about.

Given Mrs. Mawson's stubbornness, I decided it was better to consent than to contest, but the tour ended up very disappointing. Once inside the walls, she vetoed my suggested tour, wanting only to see the city's museums. No other aspect of the city interested her even slightly. In the end it was I who followed her as she decided where we would go and when.

After having lunch in a restaurant of her choice, we visited another couple of museums. Then, sated, Mrs. Mawson was finished with Siena.

As we drove back into Chianti, I reminded them of the video presentation. With a panicked look at his watch, Mr. Mawson said he'd be glad to see it—if it wasn't too long and my house wasn't too far away. I said, "We will reach my house in approximately seventeen minutes, and the video runs exactly twenty-three minutes and forty seconds." I was of course teasing.

"Good," he said, nodding his head and taking me quite seriously, "that'll let me get to the pool in time." He appeared to relax somewhat.

After fifteen minutes he became anxious again and began interrogating me with increasing alarm: "How much farther? . . . It's already been seventeen minutes . . . Shouldn't we be there by now? You said we'd be there by now . . . ," and so on, and so on. In my opinion he was behaving less like a prominent bank manager than a spoiled child.

Finally we reached the house, and I wasted no time popping the video into the machine. But after just a few minutes, when they had only seen some of the preparations for the Palio and nothing of the race—or even the trials!—Mr. Mawson stood up, looked at his watch, and said, "Very good, very interesting. But now it's time for my dip." Whereupon he left the house and stood waiting by the van.

Completely demoralized, I drove them back to the hotel. While we were en route, I noticed that the sky was darkening rapidly; rather nastily, I hoped it might rain and ruin my client's bathing plans.

And sure enough, no more than a few minutes after I'd dropped them off, the first drops fell. I smiled in satisfaction— then laughed, as those few drops were succeeded by a memorable storm. Some pagan rain god had heard my wish, and granted it. With pleasure, I imagined Mr. Mawson watching the storm from his hotel window, continually checking his watch and saying to no one in particular, "Very good, very refreshing. But this has to stop now; it's past time for my dip."

The following morning, when I flung open the window, I was greeted by a very deep, bruised-black sky, in which enormous rain clouds careened about in swollen splendor. I had seldom seen a morning sky quite so dark, and I have to say it was rather alarming. I took a deep breath, and my lungs filled with humidity and static electricity.

Despite the ill-omened sky, I was obligated to go and collect the Mawsons for a morning tour of Crete, after which I would accompany them to the station where they would catch their train to Rome.

Not long after we left Siena, while we were on the road to Asciano with its panorama of lunar landscapes, the sky cracked open and it began to pour as I had never known it to before. The downpour was so heavy that I couldn't see more than a yard ahead, and the pounding on the car was just shy of deafening. In no time the fields and the roads were completely flooded. In the backseat Mrs. Mawson sat rigid with fear, while next to me in the passenger seat, her husband intensified his watch-checking tic to the point at which his head pivoted like a metronome. I tried to reassure them, saying that the thunderstorm would soon blow over, and that it wouldn't affect our plans because our first stop would be indoors, at a monastery. I continued driving, creeping along and chatting happily, pretending that all was okay, even as the dirt road beneath me was morphing into a slick river of mud. I reflected that if the van skidded off the road, God only knew how long we would have to wait before someone would come along to help, this being such a desolate part of the country.

Finally we passed through the very worst of the storm and were in sight of our first destination. But Mr. Mawson, who was visibly shaken—whether by the force of the storm or by the fact that it had thrown us off schedule—asked me suddenly, "What exactly is there to see in this monastery?"

"Well," I said, a little abashed, "you'll be able to admire the splendid fifteenth-century frescoes painted by famous artists such as Luca Signorelli and Antonio Bazzi."

He shook his head. "That's enough. I'm tired of looking at Madonnas. I don't want to stop in Monte Oliveto."

I explained that in none of the frescoes that surround the cloister was there any trace of a Madonna, and that even if he wasn't interested, it made sense to stop at least to shelter from the rain and wait for the weather to improve. Very annoyed, he asked me what else I had in store for them that day. I said that we would visit a winery where we would have lunch, then visit the abbey of Sant'Antimo to listen to the monks chant; finally, if it had stopped raining, we would walk through Montalcino before heading to the train station.

He considered all of this for a while, then inexplicably boomeranged back to his original objection: "No, enough Madonnas. I've had it!"

For the first time in my career as a tour guide, I felt stuck. The rain was beating on the windshield, my client was refusing to go on, and his embarrassed and frightened wife sat behind us, uttering not a word. I pulled over to the side of the road and, in a firm voice, said, "Tell me what you want me to do."

"I want to go immediately to Rome," he said. I pointed out that he had reserved tickets on a train for five in the afternoon and that it was at present only ten in the morning. "I don't care," he shot back. "Take us to the station; we'll catch the first available train!"

With a sigh I turned the car around and slowly made my way back along the road—difficult to maneuver at the best of times because of its sharp curves, but now almost impassable due to the positive onslaught of the weather. When we reached the bottom of the valley, we passed some small villages that had been completely flooded and saw many cars that had been forced to stop because the water had risen above the level of their tires. Fortunately my mini van's four-wheel drive allowed us to continue. Neither my passengers nor, by this time, I myself could wait to reach the station in Chiusi.

Despite it being obvious that I had to concentrate while driving in these conditions, Mr. Mawson kept peppering me with questions: "How much longer? . . . What time will we arrive? . . ." Always checking, rechecking his watch.

On the square in front of the station, I quarreled with a traffic warden who—never mind that it was raining cats and dogs—did not allow me to stop in front of the main entrance long enough to unload the luggage. Once inside, wet and frustrated and exhausted by the drive, I noticed that due to the flooding many trains were running late; the first train for Rome wasn't for more than an hour. I was not to be rid of the Mawsons as soon as I'd thought.

To pass the time we sat down for coffee—and to my astonishment, the couple started raving about the enjoyable days we'd passed together, heaping me with praise that seemed utterly sincere and, before leaving me, handing me a very generous tip. Mr. Mawson said that I seemed to be an honest, intelligent, and generous person (a few minutes before, I'd handed a few bills to a Gypsy girl begging at the tables) and that he would've liked to have a son like me. I certainly could have predicted none of this.

As they boarded the train, I waved good-bye—and an enfeebled sun started at last to peer out from behind the clouds. While I drove back home, I saw that the storm had passed; but I also saw, very clearly now, all the damage it had inflicted, and I realized that it had been truly unwise to drive through that near maelstrom. As if to bring home this epiphany, I saw that one of the bridges we'd crossed that morning had collapsed. I could not repress a shudder. Perhaps the rain god I had invoked the night before had responded with excessive zeal; or perhaps it was his intention to punish me for having wished him on Mr. Mawson. Whatever the case, I decided never again to call on him. At least, not until my next difficult customer decides he wants a swim.

STRANGERS IN A STRANGE LAND

One of my greatest worries at the beginning of my new career was whether I was capable of dealing closely with people from countries whose tastes, customs, and traditions were unfamiliar to me. After all, I'd spent the previous ten years among exclusively local people—my colorful colleagues in the Cecchi wine cellars and the nonconformist friends with whom I made my wild country raids.

From now on I would instead have to deal not only with new people but many different kinds of new people, and this both worried and intrigued me. What's more, my decision to limit myself to very small groups would make my relationships with these people more intense and intimate—as opposed, say, to the kind of tour guide who shepherds whole busloads of faceless tourists hither and yon.

To avoid the temptation of second-guessing my clients' tastes and desires, I imposed on myself a strict rule: During my tours I would always be myself and avoid hiding behind any kind of mask. I must say that in this case sincerity has worked beautifully. In ten years of guiding, during which I have accompanied people from every part of the world and of every social rank, I have (with a few exceptions of mutual aversion) been so comfortable with my clients that at the end of the day they almost always pass directly into the category of friends.

Lunch is definitely the moment at which my contact with my customers is closest. As such, this is usually the time to help the more distracted among them learn my name correctly. Over the years both my Christian name and my family name have suffered many interesting interpretations. *Dario* in most cases becomes *Mario,* a much more common Italian name in the United States; or else *Derrio,* which is as close as some Americans can come to the true pronunciation. Among the more classically trained, it evolves into the Latin *Darius.*

My last name, *Castagno* (Italian for "chestnut"), proves even more difficult, because the pronunciation of the *gn* seems quite simply to thwart Anglo-Saxon tongues. In Italian, *gn* is pronounced *ny*—as in *Ca-sta-nyo.* (When I was a child in England, my peers usually called me *Kastag-no,* with sounds something like a comic-book sound effect.) Fortunately, when in doubt some people resort to diminutives like *Cas* or *Kes* or *Stag,* which are acceptable and even endearing—and certainly better than those who insist on saying *Castagna,* or the gentleman who in a public square kept calling "Gestapo! Gestapo!" while growing annoyed that I wouldn't answer him.

Perhaps the most unendurable types are those who, not having grasped either of my names, decide wittily to use one of their own invention. Often these people call me *Tony,* as though in Italy we are all christened Antonio. The most amusing such variation came from a distinguished gentleman from Washington, who, despite my having introduced myself as Dario, spent an entire morning calling me "Louie." When we were seated for lunch, I finally asked why he was using that name instead of my own. He looked perplexed and said, "But this morning at the hotel desk, I asked who my guide was, and the receptionist pointed at you and said, 'Louie.'" I explained that *lui* is Italian for "him."

Usually for lunch I book a restaurant managed by my friend Gina and her daughter Carla, who reserve me a table in their private garden, beneath the shade of an old maple tree, from which we have a view of the rolling Chianti hills. Gina is a genuine Chianti personality who treats me as if I were her son, and for me she is indeed a second mother. Of typically robust Tuscan humor, she can summon up such reserves of sunny good cheer as to make even a condemned man smile, then just a day later retreat behind a wall so high that anyone who didn't know her would believe she was in mourning. The Gina I prefer is definitely the former, who throws open her arms at the sight of me and cries, *"Darino, il mio bambino!"* then sits me down and tells me all her amusing news, finally clapping her hands together and musically exclaiming "Mamma mia!"—which sends my customers into transports because it is so typically Italian. My guests adore her and often send me photos and notes to deliver to her. Both Gina and Carla—worthy heir to her mother both in temperament and in the kitchen—love to stuff me and my customers with their genuine homemade food.

As in any respectable Tuscan restaurant, lunch begins with a tray of *crostini*—little slices of toasted bread spread with sauce. When these arrive on the table, Americans almost invariably exclaim, "Ah, *bruschetta!*"—and I must point out that a *bruschetta* is usually larger than a *crostino* and flavored only with garlic, oil, and salt. The variety of sauces found on *crostini,* on the other hand, is wide ranging; you'll find them made with chicken livers or spleen, fresh tomato and basil, porcini mushrooms, mayonnaise and garlic, parsley and other aromatic herbs, and so on.

After the *crostini* disappear (usually quickly), my customers wipe their mouths and say, "Thanks Dario, great lunch. Where to now?" Lunch? But lunch has only just begun! Now comes a steaming *ribollita,* followed by a tray of homemade ravioli, then some pasta with zucchini, quickly succeeded by stewed wild boar . . . and then you're ready for the main course: beefsteak with porcini mushrooms and roasted vegetables. And to wash it all down, an honest *fiasco* of the house wine. By this time you should have achieved your second wind—so out comes Carla's homemade *tiramisù.* And afterward, to aid the digestion, a shot of grappa.

When I announce this extravagant menu, many of my customers think I'm joking. Then the food comes—and comes—and comes—and they just hunker down and enjoy it all. With our bellies full and a little wine loosening our tongues, we can get to know each other better. Suddenly I find myself answering all kinds of questions on topics that range far afield of Chianti and its pleasures—including the curious and often indecipherable habits of the Italians, the political landscape of the country at present, even the phenomenon of the Mafia in Sicily.

The most common question by far is, "Do you eat like this every day?" To which I answer, Sure—why should I do otherwise? "But surely you don't have dinner, then." Of course I do! It would be a crime to go to bed with an empty stomach. "So how is it that in Italy people eat so much but hardly anyone's overweight?" To tell you the truth, this has always been a mystery to me, but I feel obliged to offer my clients a few observations. It's true that in Italy we eat enormous lunches and also a rather substantial dinner, but our breakfast is practically nonexistent, composed of a cappuccino and a roll at most, and very rarely will we snack between meals. Whereas the impression I've formed of America is that a great deal of snacking goes on—in cars, on the job, at movie theaters, watching television—everywhere and at any time of day. Then there's the kind of food that's being consumed: all those fast foods and packaged snacks loaded with fat and sugar. It's true, we Italians eat more when we sit down at the table, but it's also true that if the calories of all the day's meals were added up, our diet isn't so rich as it seems. Above all, our main dressing, extra-virgin olive oil, is easier to digest and lower in saturated fat than the butter or lard so often used in the States. I'm not a nutritionist, but I believe that these differences must have some bearing on Italians' overall health. We walk a lot here, too, even in the country. That's got to have some effect.

Another question I'm often asked is why, after having drunk red wine in Italy, you don't suffer headaches, while in the United States, many of my customers have had to give it up entirely because of the terrible morning-after throbbing. Again I have no answer, only a theory: I believe that the American headache is provoked by the excess of sulfites, a substance that in the U.S. is required by law to be added in certain percentages to all wines (even imports) for preservation. The level of sulfites in Italy is, I'm certain, much lower.

Sometimes my clients' questions edge into the bizarre. A man from New York once asked in all seriousness where the Tower of Pisa is. I told him it was in Pisa. He looked astonished, then abashed. After a visit to Siena, one small group from Ohio asked why the city had been "built uphill." With a slight tinge of irony, I replied, "It's only built half uphill. The other half is all downhill." They shook their heads. "We've only seen the steep parts. Can you show us on the map where it starts going down?" Another lady, from Atlanta, asked why everyone was speaking

Italian. What other answer could I give her?—"Because we are in Italy."

One client completely confounded me by asking me where in Siena "Piocsi Street" was located. She'd seen something there she wanted to return to, and made a note of the name. There is, I told her, no Piocsi Street in Siena—nothing even close. Angered by my apparent stupidity, she pestered me about my lack of knowledge until, quite by chance, we happened across the street during our tour—Via Pio XI, the boulevard named after Pope Pius the Eleventh.

Perhaps my favorite such inquiry came from a client who, while examining a map of Italy during a country drive, asked me whether many kangaroos made it "over the border." I thought for a moment but couldn't imagine what he meant, so I told him we were unlikely to see any. It was only later, refolding the map he'd left lying open on the van's backseat, that I noticed what he'd done: confused our neighbor Austria with a country much, *much* farther away.

After the confounding questions there are the unanswerable observations that always seem to come in conflicting pairs. "It seems like everyone in Italy owns a dog," one client will note. The next day, another will ask, "Why don't Italians have any dogs?" A client will congratulate me on our well-kept, well-marked roads; the next day one of his countrymen will ask why no one takes care of the roads and why all the signs are so misleading. "Why are all the women here so beautiful?" asks one. "What makes Italian women so ugly?" asks another. "You have such sophisticated men here." "Are all Italian men so vulgar and badly dressed?" "Italians are so friendly—everyone is eager to give you a hand." "Why do your people just sneer at me when I ask them for help?"

It's easy—and perhaps natural—to make such generalizations. Who hasn't, while traveling, made the mistake of judging an entire nation based on the behavior of a few individual citizens? Yet as a native, I can't help feeling abused. Many times I've had clients unfavorably judge the Sienese because of the curt service of one or two waiters; but how many Sienese work as waiters? . . . And of those few, how many are genuinely Sienese? In fact, many restaurant workers these days are immigrants. Do I bring this up, at the risk of seeming combative? Or do I try harder to balance my clients' hastily made opinions with further sights, sounds, and experiences? . . . Usually, of course, the latter.

This brings to mind a phenomenon I have confronted time and again, which is that, in Italy, service people "mirror" the people they are serving—assuming the attitudes and behaviors of their customers. For this reason, pushy, rude foreigners will complain that the Italians are discourteous; demanding visitors will go home and say that the Italians are unhelpful; loud people will find the Italians obnoxious; while, of course, polite, open-minded travelers will invariably be enchanted by us.

One pair of customers, after we had spent a pleasant day together, asked me to recommend an elegant place for dinner. I reserved them a table at a friend's restaurant, where I was certain they would find good food and attentive service. Everyone I'd ever sent there had come back raving about it. So I was astonished when I picked them up the next day and found them still fuming over the terrible experience they'd had the night before. They had quarreled with the staff and nearly come to blows with the owner, with the result that at the end of the discussion the chef himself had kicked them out.

I couldn't believe my ears; my friend would not have behaved this way! I was very upset and angry, and as soon as the tour concluded, I rushed into town to scold him. I found him in the back room sipping a glass of Prosecco. When I started to berate him, he waved me into a chair, told me to relax and poured me a glass, then proceeded to tell me what had happened the previous evening.

My clients had reserved a table for nine o'clock but arrived two hours later, when the restaurant was empty and the kitchen was closing. The owner, knowing that they were my customers, had gone out of his way to be polite, had recalled the waiter (who had already changed and was ready to go home), and presented his extravagant menu, from which it's possible to order more than sixty different plates and hundreds of excellent wines.

"The *signori*," my beleaguered friend continued, "asked me all sorts of questions about the composition of the plates, and I patiently described them one by one. Around midnight they finally made their decision, and do you know what they ordered?" I couldn't imagine what, from his own menu, would make him so angry. "A cappuccino, a green salad, and a bottle of mineral water! Were they crazy? I was of course very offended; all the same I tried to keep calm, and with as much politeness as possible, I told them that they could easily have found such things in the snack bar next door." He broke off his narrative momentarily, because in his agitation he had allowed the wine to choke him slightly. After he'd finished coughing he resumed. "I can assure you, those two were taking the piss out of me! That woman turning her face up so angelically as she ordered her coffee, asking me the word for 'cappuccino' in Italian. I'd had enough, and invited them politely to leave."

I tried to explain to him that the question was not at all ironic, since many foreigners are now so accustomed to drinking cappuccino in their own countries that they don't realize it's actually an Italian creation. But I could see that he wasn't listening. "Anyhow," he continued, "when I asked them to leave, she began screaming at me, saying that in Italy we are all rude bastards and Mafiosi, and she threw the water bottle on the floor! She was completely hysterical. Then her husband accused me of having upset his wife, and between one insult and another, they yanked the tablecloth off, upsetting all the dishes and cutlery. At that point Mario"—the restaurant's gigantic Sicilian chef—"who was already miffed because he'd been made to stay late, came out of the kitchen and actually pushed them both out into the street. *Ecco*," he concluded sadly, "that's how it went."

Humbled, I swallowed the Prosecco and left.

Thus we are left with an American couple who will spend the rest of their lives vilifying all Italians, based on a single experience in which they—perhaps even innocently—pushed a single Italian beyond his limit. Not every cross-cultural clash is so explosive, of course, just as not all American visitors to my friend's restaurant risk making the acquaintance of Mario. But I am constantly on my guard that such things are possible. I recognized very early that I had made it my life's work to usher people from one part of the world through another—a place where the customs are new to them, the language unfamiliar, the traditions strange, and where a salad can serve as an insult.

But without risk there is no reward. On balance I think my efforts have, in their own small way, been of some benefit to Italo-American relations.

OCTOBER AND THE COACH TOUR

Now comes the high point of the year: the grape harvest, or *vendemmia*. The air fills with the aroma of the crushed fruit, then of the musk as it begins to ferment in the vats.

Chianti is rich in wild crops. Blackberry bushes grow everywhere, as do fat juicy sloes, chestnuts, juniper berries, mushrooms, and even hazelnuts. Especially abundant are acorns, a favorite delicacy among the many wild boars, and of the jays, whose harsh call is often heard ripping through the woods. Near the farmhouses, walnut and fig trees are common, the latter often, incredibly, rooting within cracks in the walls.

The autumn colors are only just ripening, and during the day the sun is still warm, though at sunset cold can settle suddenly, leaving us no illusions: Summer is over. This is the moment to set a match to the fireplace, roast chestnuts, and lay in a store of firewood for the long winter ahead.

Some months before the tourist season, I was contacted by an amicable middle-aged woman who was traveling through Italy with her husband. They were inspecting a few sites around which they would organize a tour that fall. She asked if I could accompany her for three days in the Sienese area, to show her what I thought was most important to see.

It was February, not usually the most comfortable month for a tour, but we were very fortunate, finding ourselves enjoying the kind of brilliantly clear winter days that allow you to perceive on the distant horizon things that are obscured during the rest of the year.

It was probably because my clients were such easy company, or maybe because I was so relaxed—this being in the midst of my usual winter hibernation—but I found those three days spent together particularly pleasant. Even so, Mrs. Ames worked very hard, asking me for many explanations and tips and taking down an incredible number of notes and observations, while her husband, who evidently was there only to accompany her, sat in the backseat serenely smoking his cigars.

At the end of the third day, Mrs. Ames invited me to the hotel bar. Sipping an aperitif, she said she liked the way I worked, and wondered whether I would be willing to conduct a tour using the same itinerary she and her husband had enjoyed, only this time for twenty people. She was arranging this tour on behalf of a Miss Morrison, and one of her promises to Miss Morrison was to find a suitable guide.

I was stymied. If I accepted, I would be going against my espoused ideal of tourism, and the whole *raison d'être* of Rooster Tours—intimate, easygoing tours for no more than five or six. But if I said no, I would perhaps offend Mrs. Ames, and would feel obliged to help her find a replacement, of which I really know none. After nearly an hour of my hedging and her pleading, I finally accepted, with one ironclad condition: The guests—all twenty of them—would have to follow the established program.

Despite the ready submission of Mrs. Ames to this demand, I began, a few days later, to receive from Miss Morrison a whole series of faxes in which she asked dozens of questions about the itinerary and asked repeatedly about inserting some extra stops.

She wanted to know if during the morning of the first day I would meet them in Florence, join them on their bus and entertain the group during the trip to San Gimignano, then continue to Siena for our tour of the city, and in the evening have dinner in Montalcino before returning to Siena and their hotel. The following day she ordered up visits to Montepulciano, Montalcino, Pienza, the Banfi winery and museum, the small Barbi farm, the Monastery of Monte Oliveto—and all of these to be concluded in time to hear the famous Gregorian chants at the Abbey of Sant'Antimo. The third day was to include, by her demand, not only the tour of Chianti that I had proposed but also a cooking class held by a famous noble Italian lady well known in the United States for her gourmet lessons on TV.

Not content to inflict these marathon days on her friends, she expected me to book them mammoth meals for each lunch and dinner, in very elegant and exclusive restaurants. *Here we go again*, I thought. *I have the impression that we will be soon forced to have a chat.* And indeed, what ensued was a long correspondence via fax in which I succeeded—at least in part—in convincing her that her program simply wasn't possible, given the immutable laws of physics. In order to do everything she wanted, we would need to be in at least two places at once, possibly three. Accordingly, we would have to modify.

After seven months of seemingly endless adjustments, the definitive program was finally set.

The first day we would leave Florence and go directly to Siena, visit the city, and have lunch in a typical *enoteca*; in the afternoon I would accompany them to their hotel, where they would rest. In the evening, contrary to my advice, they would have dinner in a renowned but very distant restaurant, at least an hour and a half from Siena by bus.

The second day I would accompany them to the Monastery of Monte Oliveto, then to a winery that produces the famous Brunello, and then to Montalcino. For lunch I suggested stopping in a very typical place, as a change from the elegant nouvelle cuisine that Miss Morrison had arranged for all the other meals.

The third day we would go directly to the cooking lesson, where we would also have lunch; in the afternoon I would accompany them on an improvised tour of Chianti, for whatever amount of time remained.

I was dreading this group. Even though they wouldn't arrive till October, I started worrying at the beginning of the season, and every time I thought about them thereafter, I immediately felt a lead weight settle in my stomach. The closer the day got, the worse my anxiety. Finally, it arrived.

The departure from Florence was established for eight thirty. Therefore I had to be awake at five, to catch the bus that would get me to their hotel in time. Walking through the quiet streets of Florence from the bus station, as the city slowly shrugged off sleep and started preparing for a new day, I tried to prepare psychologically.

At the hotel I found the bus driver, a good-hearted young Roman named Nando whom, as it happened, I had met before. I passed the time chatting with him.

At eight thirty, the preordained departure time, the only person who had come down to the bus was my old client, Mrs. Ames, this time without her husband. It was nine thirty before the remainder of the guests started to appear, and as I feared, they were all a bit elderly and enfeebled.

Arriving dead last was the group leader, the dreaded Miss Morrison, an enormous middle-aged woman, well over 200 pounds. Her hair was disfigured by a ridiculous perm made up of hundreds of tiny, tight curls, all a vibrant shade of red never to be found in nature. On her face she had spread a layer of an excessively deep rose makeup, unfortunately very close to the hue she had chosen for her lipstick, so that at first glance she looked as though she had no lips at all. She wore an elegant green dress, completely unsuitable for a country tour, while her feet were shod courtesy of the ubiquitous Nike. I introduced myself and shook her hand, and was almost thrown off balance by the weight of her arm, loaded as it was with cumbersome gold bracelets.

She boarded the bus and made the roll call, and then with a *clackety-clack* of jewelry gestured to Nando to get rolling. Once we were on the road, I took the microphone. After introducing myself I started telling some amusing anecdotes about the rivalry between Siena and Florence, and of my own scarce love for the Florentines.

Over my many years in this line of work, I've come to rely on these anecdotes as a way to break the ice. The customer giggles or chuckles, and immediately we both feel more at ease. This time, not one of my twenty clients as much as smiled.

Near eleven we reached Siena. I decided the best plan of action was to disembark the bus at the ancient Porta Romana, cross the historical center on foot, then get back on the coach—which in the meantime would drive around to the opposite wall of the city and thus be there waiting for us.

The moment we got off the bus, everyone began asking, "How much do we have to walk?" I explained that if we were to visit Siena we would have to walk, because the center of the city is closed to automobiles. Every hundred yards or so, I had to stop and wait for the slowest to catch up, and despite maintaining an achingly slow pace myself, I somehow managed to keep pulling away from the group. Every two minutes someone would call out, "How much farther do we have to walk?" After twenty minutes, and as many pauses, we reached the Campo. My explanation of the Palio's role in Sienese life and the significance of the surrounding monuments was peppered by the exhausted groans, moans, and stifled yawns of my customers. At the end of my spiel, I asked if anyone had any questions. One woman asked which was the best hairdresser in town and could I get her an appointment; another wanted to know where she could buy a bar of chocolate and a Coke.

This depressing moment on the square was followed by an even less successful visit to the Duomo. Inside the vastness of the cathedral, my clients listlessly looked about them in the most perfunctory manner, as though they were turning their heads merely because they were meant to. No one seemed interested in the slightest degree in anything I had to say or show them.

For lunch I took them to my favorite wine cellar; they consumed the meal in total silence. I sat next to Miss Morrison, who wanted to know what menu I had fixed for lunch the following day in Montalcino. I said that because they had been eating in rather exclusive, nouvelle cuisine restaurants, I had arranged a typically Tuscan experience for contrast—*bruschette*, bean soup, a variety of mixed grilled meats and vegetables, and some *cantuccini* biscuits to dip in the *vin santo* to finish off. She looked at me, flabbergasted, and ordered me to change the menu at once: The "bruschella" would never suit her guests, the bean soup must be replaced by a mushroom soup, in place of the mixed meats I was to order them to prepare rabbit, and I was to make sure the house wine was served because the Brunello was much too expensive. Never mind that Montalcino is the home of that superb vintage.

While she spoke I noticed that her plump cheeks had become a more intense shade of pink—perhaps due to the effort of the walk, or perhaps I was beginning to know her better and her unpleasant character was rendering her even less attractive in my eyes. To avoid any kind of confrontation with her, I phoned the restaurant in Montalcino and passed on the new instructions. After lunch, despite the total indifference of the group, I took them to see the private museum of a *contrada*, after which we began the walk to the coach.

When we had gone just a few hundred yards, some of my guests were too tired to continue and forced me to call them some taxis. Without commenting, I did as I was told, but I suspect that my expression in that moment may have been more eloquent than mere words. When, finally, we all had reached the coach, I put my disappointment behind me and bade them good-bye with a smile, wishing them well until I saw them again the next day.

I arrived at the hotel at around eight the next morning, and Nando filled me in on what had happened at dinner the night before.

The group had left Siena very late, ignoring the established timetable. Since the restaurant Miss Morrison had chosen was south of Montalcino, the drive took an eternity, and by the time the group had arrived there, dined, and returned to the hotel, it was well past two in the morning. I laughed; it had gone exactly as I'd predicted. Nando looked perplexed when I told him we'd be going back to Montalcino that very day. "If they were so keen on hitting that restaurant," he asked in his marked Roman accent, "couldn't they just have had lunch there today instead of taking that long trek last night?" I agreed that would have been the logical thing to do, but what had logic to do with Miss Morrison?

Once again, all the guests were forty-five minutes late in arriving and boarding, but after having heard about their misadventure the night before, I'd expected as much.

As soon as we left Siena and were on a deserted side road, the first request of the day was made: Someone had an urgent need for a pharmacy. Because we wouldn't see any more pharmacies until we reached Montalcino, we were forced turn back to Siena, where the afflicted customer bought some pills for carsickness.

We got under way again and soon found ourselves on the panoramic road that crosses the evocative hills of the Crete Senesi. During the drive I provided exhaustive information on the day's itinerary as well as on the historical background of our first stop, with no one paying any attention whatsoever. When we arrived in Monte Oliveto, we disembarked the coach, crossed the suspension bridge, and passed through the arched entrance dominated by two splendid figures carved by Della Robbia. While I was pointing out to the group the wonders of those sculptures, I noticed that most of them were far more interested in the sign that indicated the direction of the toilets.

After a seemingly infinite break for this important visit, we descended the steep, cypress-lined road that leads to the monastery. Here I led the group through the series of frescoes of Signorelli and Il Sodoma that fill the walls of the beautiful cloister with scenes from the life of Saint Benedict. They were painted in the fifteenth century and are spectacular works of rare beauty—in my opinion they are the artistic treasures of this area.

The group began this part of the tour bored and inattentive . . . and then they got worse. I quickly noticed that some of them were taking flash pictures, despite the very visible signs prohibiting this. I put a stop to it, but just a few moments later had to chide someone who, while asking about one of the scenes, had indicated which one it was by laying his finger on it. Finally I had to resort to shouting when a certain lady decided to rest her travel-weary frame by leaning up against one of the frescoes. I was upset; I was dealing with a group of older, supposedly respectable people who were behaving exactly like a class of children on a school field trip.

As soon as we left the cloister, Miss Morrison made a beeline for me. I smelled her before I saw her, the thick cloud of sickly sweet scent assailing me well in advance of her person—thus giving me time quickly to grimace, then adjust my features.

"Dario," she said, smiling as pleasantly as she could, "may I borrow your phone for a moment?" I handed it over. She moved away to make her call, and it was only when her miasma had dissipated and I could once again think clearly that I became aware that she was calling Nando. I could hear her ordering him to drive the bus down the hill to collect us, so that the slothful group wouldn't have to walk back up to the parking lot. "Excuse me," I said, leaping into action, "you can't ask the bus to come down here! First of all, it's prohibited, and with good reason—the road is too narrow. I really don't think it's worth getting fined, or getting stuck, just to avoid a few yards' walk!"

But Miss Morrison was unmovable. Poor Nando was forced to drive down the tree-lined avenue, where he damaged some cypresses—and as I'd foretold, he could hardly maneuver. When the exhaust gases began to fill up the inside of the church, the monks, who to that moment had pretended not to see any-thing, came forth, threatening to call the police if we didn't leave immediately.

Because of this we had to skip the visit to the abbey's Benedictine pharmacy, where the tourists could have purchased some of the liniments, salves, and other products made on the premises by the monks. Since the only activity they were ever keen on was shopping, this was a hard blow for the group, and many began to show signs of impatience with their leader.

Our next stop was the Barbi vineyard, maker of the leg-endary Brunello di Montalcino. We lunched in their restaurant on the menu I'd adjusted the day before with Miss Morrison. She astonished me by introducing it to the others as "typically Tuscan." Because she had refused the *bruschetta* appetizer, we passed directly to the mushroom soup, a rather peculiar dish that in fact was only appreciated by a few in the party. When the main course—stewed rabbit—arrived, I heard some screams of horror from many of the tables: Apparently no one was willing to eat poor "Bugs Bunny."

Anarchy loomed. To prevent it I stood up and announced that we were just joking; in fact the dish was a kind of local chicken. Fortunately they believed me and eagerly cleaned their plates, downing it all with the more economical Rosso di Montalcino Miss Morrison had chosen instead of the Brunello. Very likely all the money she saved passed directly into her pockets, because no tourist who comes to Montalcino misses tasting the Brunello, even if it is a bit expensive.

Back on the bus, we continued toward Sant'Antimo, the abbey where we would hear the monks in plainsong. During this short hop the ever-constant Miss Morrison called me over and in a firm voice announced a change in the itinerary: After the chanting we would, instead of visiting Montalcino, head to Pienza. As she said this, she pulled out her lurid pink lipstick, pursed her lips, and touched up her Halloween-style makeup. "Signora," I said, "Pienza is indeed a jewel, but since you've made your guests come to Montalcino twice in two days and they still haven't visited the town, it would seem more logical to stop there first."

As soon as the word *logical* escaped my lips, I knew I had chosen the wrong argument for Miss Morrison. And sure enough, she remained fixed on her change of plan. But I had spent the entire day providing exhaustive explanations on the wine industry and the history of Montalcino, and I wasn't about to have all that work go for nothing. Suddenly I remembered those ripples of bad feeling Miss Morrison had stirred up after she'd gotten us kicked out of Monte Oliveto. With this in mind I decided to try another plan.

"All right," I said, "because you're all Americans, and because the United States is the world's largest democracy, let's put it to a vote." A show of hands revealed a preference for Montalcino— perhaps to thwart Miss Morrison, perhaps because the group had figured out that going to Pienza meant returning to Siena much later.

Thus, after having heard the monks, we stopped in Montalcino, one of the best-known and most characteristically medieval towns of Tuscany. But it had been forced on Miss Morrison, and she was not to be placated by its charms. "We can only stop here for fifteen minutes," she insisted—ridiculously, as she had previously been willing to commit us to the much more time-consuming journey to Pienza.

Now, Montalcino is not a big place, but not even the Olympic sprinter Michael Johnson in peak condition would be able to see much of it in so short a period. The group did as much as it could within the time constraints, but many were afraid to wander far lest they be unable to return to the bus in time.

When everyone had returned, Miss Morrison, still doing a slow burn over losing the vote, said into her microphone, "This town is just horrible! What a waste of time!" In other words: *Never force your personal desires on me again, or I'll ruin it for you.* The return trip to Siena passed in almost total silence.

At home that evening I felt utterly decimated; my only consolation was that I had but one day left with the group. In the morning, when I saw Nando looking as morally and physically exhausted as I was, I told him how sorry I was for him—it was my last day, but he had to put up with those people for another week and a half.

Scheduled for this day was what was supposed to be the highlight of the whole tour: a cooking class held in the rooms of an ancient castle. I was also eager to attend because so many of my customers had spoken about this chef and her popular TV show.

When we reached the castle, there was a bit of confusion: We were made to go on a brief tour of the premises before taking our places inside the immense, ancient kitchen. I noticed with interest that the members of my group seemed at last interested and alert. They watched avidly as the noble chef whipped up a chocolate cake, stuffed crepes, and chicken breasts with a rosemary sauce. In order to prepare the vegetables for browning, she pulled out the appropriate half-moon-shaped mincing knife. The *mezzaluna* is a very common instrument in Italian kitchens, an absolutely everyday object for us, but it provoked astonished exclamations among the audience.

Suddenly they came wildly alive. From their bags they

pulled out cameras and videocams they hadn't touched in all the days prior, and the room was immediately illuminated by volleys of flashbulbs, crazily strobing the walls and ceiling as though a celebrity had just walked in. I would never have dreamed that of all the monuments, abbeys, cities, vineyards, and artworks I had shown the group, a simple mincing knife would be the thing that finally ravished them.

When the meal was ready, the noble lady led us into a splendid hall where waiters had set two round wooden tables in a very elegant way. At the first table sat half of the tourists with our hostess-chef, while the rest of us were placed with the chef's husband. As soon as we were seated, I tried to engage this man in conversation, but became quickly aware that he had some kind of affliction; instead of answering my questions, he kindly smiled and nodded his head up and down.

The meal was delicious, but we were a bit embarrassed by what to do with the husband; was it kinder to let him be, or to try to talk to him and risk mortifying him if he was unable to reply? The awkwardness continued when he accompanied us into the garden for coffee.

Finally we said good-bye to this odd noble couple and returned to the coach. As soon as we boarded, Miss Morrison seized my arm and said, "Dario, we've got to skip the visit to Castle Brolio and just go to Radda." Even though I thought it a pity to skip the castle in favor of the town, I knew it would be futile to argue; besides, I was beginning to fear for my arm. I consented, and she released me.

When we reached Radda she granted her party another fifteen minutes of freedom, which in this case proved sufficient, given the small size and scarcity of attractions there. When the group returned their duplicitous organizer couldn't wait to pronounce Radda a delight—"What a wonderful village! Isn't it so much nicer than Montalcino?"

As the tourists returned to their seats, I noticed that all of them—and I mean each and every one—had taken the opportunity to purchase a *mezzaluna*.

Fortunately the day was now over. When we returned to Siena, I said good-bye to the group. I didn't receive a single coin as a tip, but Miss Morrison did bestow upon me her litany of criticisms, which she must have thought were worth more to me than money. "You have a great knowledge of the territory," she said loftily, "but your attitude is very unpleasant and you don't take orders well. However, despite everything, I will send you other customers."

I tried to imagine the kinds of people she would send my way—more herds of bovine, incurious, humorless nonentities led by Miss Morrison's equally lacquered and tyrannical colleagues. I thanked her, but said for my part I would accept no such referrals, then turned and left her in a state of sputtering confusion.

As I walked away, I had a strong urge to turn back, go right up to her, and squeeze those plump pink cheeks between my fingers—but the urge passed, and I was left feeling nothing but a kind of pity for her.

After some weeks I was astonished to receive a letter in which the crazy Miss Morrison thanked me on behalf of all her guests for three memorable days they would always treasure. I thought about it for a while, and decided that, in the end, the *mezzaluna* had saved me.

INTERVALLO

Death and Life in America

On a spectacularly mild October day, I went to pick up a Mr. and Mrs. Hanley, who had rented a rather remote house atop a hill overlooking one of the most beautiful valleys of Chianti. To reach them my faithful four-wheel-drive van had to scramble up a steep rubble road and through a magnificent forest of chestnut trees, already turned to gold and ready to shed their precious fruits.

Though isolated, the small house was pleasant enough, having been restored with simplicity and good taste. And the vista was incredible. My customers were already waiting for me in front, by the chicken yard. We immediately hit it off, and given the brilliant sun we'd been blessed with, I was sure that we would spend a wonderful day together.

By the time we sat down for lunch, Mr. and Mrs. Hanley had become Bruce and Suzanne. But then the tone of our morning changed. Bruce had his attention distracted by a local paper a man at the next table was reading. Despite having no Italian, Bruce could see that the entire front page was devoted to the execution of an American citizen that had occurred the previous day in Virginia. Both Bruce and Suzanne asked me to confirm this, and I did so, explaining that every time an execution takes place in the United States, it echoes so loudly over here that accounts of it often occupy more than a page of the nation's major newspapers.

Suzanne was surprised but favorably impressed. She said proudly, "Bruce's job is to help defend people sentenced to death."

It was my turn to be impressed. Bruce told me that his work had lately become a kind of battle, and that even when he was sure of the guilt of a prisoner, he tried to keep him from execution, even if this forced him to travel thousands of miles and pay all the expenses out of his own pocket. "Dario," he said, shaking his head, "if you buy any of today's American papers, you won't find a single column inch about that execution. The media is totally indifferent, because sadly the public is, too."

He wasn't telling me anything new. I described to the Hanleys the tight bond that exists between Italy and the United States—a bond of which the average American is largely unaware. "Everything that happens in the U.S. is big news in Europe, because you set the standards we end up following. Ever since the war, you've influenced us on every level—from how we dress and what music we hear, to how we think about who we are. Turning on the TV here is like opening a window directly onto America: We get your films, sitcoms, soap operas, and of course the live news from CNN. Your movie stars are part of our pop culture. Your sports legends are equally legendary over here. Your presidential scandals are front-page gossip in our magazines."

Suzanne looked at me in amused disbelief. "Come on,

Dario—you make it sound like when a fly falls in America, you hear it hit the floor in Europe."

"Absolutely," I said. "And because we see the United States as a kind of big brother, many of your realities scare us. Like the free circulation of weapons and the use of capital punishment."

Our excellent lunch was being forgotten in the heat of our discussion. "Any news of an execution in the States," I continued, "is so publicized by our mass media that often I ask my clients for more information about it. And every time I do, their reaction amazes and disturbs me: Most know nothing, not even about the more recent executions, while others see capital punishment as being so normal that they're surprised we don't have it over here. I always feel obliged to explain that the only Western democracy in which such a thing still exists is America."

Bruce nodded. "That's the trouble. For many Americans capital punishment has always been around—it's just part of their reality. Whereas to the rest of the world, it's mind boggling that America, a model of freedom, still employs a mode of punishment used by tyrants and dictators . . ."

" . . . including nations the United States condemns for violations of human rights," I added. The waiter came to clear our plates; astonishingly for me, I didn't remember having finished mine. "For a European," I continued, "it's difficult to reconcile the idea of democracy with the use of capital punishment. We fear that the death penalty might contaminate some of the nobler institutions and compromise the entire structure of society."

There was another open bottle of wine on the table. When had that arrived? "Every day I go into battle on this very issue," said Bruce, "but how can I discuss it reasonably with people who insist on some ancient tribal code like 'An eye for an eye, a

tooth for a tooth'? Especially since people in America are so surrounded by crime that most people are convinced capital punishment is the only effective deterrent."

I refilled our glasses, recalling how frightened some of my
American customers become when I take them through the
dark, narrow alleys around Siena—despite my repeated assur-
ances that we're completely safe. Surely our life in Chianti is
privileged in that respect; in Italy crime outside the big cities is
virtually nonexistent. Even in the cities the greatest risk to a
tourist isn't mugging or murder—it's theft. And not by an armed
robber, but by a light-fingered pickpocket. I wouldn't be afraid
to send my seven-year-old niece alone into the nighttime streets
of Siena. "All the same, I'm convinced," I said, "that increasing
the punishment for more serious offenses doesn't at all help to
deter crime. If it did, why isn't it working?"

Bruce swirled the Chianti Classico around his glass, but I
could tell that he wasn't really looking at it. "There's another reason I hear a lot of support for capital punishment," he said, "the
expense of holding a criminal in jail for life. Now, apart from the
impossibility in any moral sense of quantifying the value of a
human life, is the cost really that high?"

This time it was Suzanne who answered: "Absolutely not.
We've proven it time and again: Every execution involves enormous judicial expenses that far outweigh the costs of prison
maintenance. And you can believe us on that point, Dario, since
we've invested a good deal of our own money meeting exactly
those kinds of expenses!"

Bruce took a swig of his wine and added, "What I think will
happen eventually is that the death penalty will fall into disuse
not for any moral reason, but for economic convenience. State
governors will explain the matter in terms of income and

expense until public opinion comes around. Financial arguments are very convincing in America."

Dessert arrived and I managed to divert our attention back to the meal. At the end of the day, I accompanied the Hanleys back to their little cottage on the hilltop and said good-bye with the promise that we would stay in touch in order to continue our discussion. I then returned to Siena, paying as much attention to the beautiful fall colors as I had paid to lunch. My mind had wandered back to what we in Italy see as America's crowning pathology. It upsets us deeply when we see, on television, free and supposedly progressive American citizens partying and toasting after having attended the execution of a man who twenty years before had killed a relative or friend. Even to Italians, the people who invented the concept of *vendetta*, this seems macabre and barbaric. In our view capital punishment remains immoral even if inflicted on the worst of serial killers. If we feel horror at the crimes of an assassin, how can we turn around and accept a homicide perpetrated by the state?

I've spoken at length about the cultural differences between Italians and Americans. Still, while those differences may amuse, confuse, endear, or vex us, none of them disturbs us in the profound way this single, overwhelming dichotomy does.

Fortunately, while people like Bruce and Suzanne exist, we have hope for America . . . and so hope for us all.

NOVEMBER AND THE DEVOTED MOTHER

The leaves explode into thousands of shades of yellow, amber, brown, rose, and crimson—the surest sign that autumn has arrived. The hues are so brilliant that the country-side seems even more beautiful than in spring. Vacationers have closed the shutters, emptied the swimming pools, and gone home. The snakes, too, retreat into hibernation, but can some-times be caught grabbing their last few opportunities to doze in the sun.

During the day you can smell the potent aroma of burning leaves, while in the evening the scent of sizzling firewood snakes up from immense Tuscan fireplaces, where chestnuts are roasted in pierced pans and meat is grilled on the glowing embers. And in November the usual kind of tourist begins to give way to something . . . different.

Couple with son, 9:00 A.M., Hotel Minerva. The normal rou-tine, I thought, closing the door behind me. The morning was warm, the sky an intense, inviting blue, and the air cool and moist—a perfect day. While driving, I passed the time by taking in the splendid forest landscapes and crimson vines.

Arriving at the hotel, I noticed at once a twenty-something

brunette sunk into a gigantic armchair. She was extremely attractive, despite the look of impatient boredom she wore as she flipped through an Italian magazine. My eyes lingered over her briefly as I approached the reception desk—the classic hardwood edifice found in every four-star hotel—where I told the concierge that I had an appointment with an American couple named Weasle.

With his professional aplomb he pointed to the very woman I'd just checked out, and said, "Mrs. Weasle is seated there in the lobby."

I was surprised. She couldn't be more than twenty-three. How old could her son possibly be? . . . With a slight feeling of alarm, I considered that I might be trapped for the day with a manic, whining toddler—or, worse, a shrieking infant.

I was considering just how potent a well-worn diaper might be in the confines of my very small van when I reached my new client. "Mrs. Weasle?" I said, extending my arm. "I'm Dario."

"Oh, Dario! Nice to meet you," she said as she clambered up from the depths of the armchair. Once on her feet, she seized my hand energetically. "My husband and my son will be right down. You know how it is with children; you always need a little extra patience."

As she chattered away, I began to relax. Apparently there would be none of the awkward pauses usually suffered while trying to make conversation for the first time. Mrs. Weasle was sufficiently talkative to carry both sides of the dialogue.

"Anyway, Mario," she said, "my name's Louise, but everyone calls me Weezie." *Weezie Weasle*, I thought; *a name straight out of Hanna-Barbera*. I grinned at this, but because she was still beaming at me, my smile wasn't out of place.

"Italy's just fantastic!" she enthused. "We've been touring for two weeks and everything's been so old and fascinating and full of history." I nodded appreciatively. I'd heard this refrain many times, from many clients. "But the thing that really stands out," she continued with a sudden show of awe, "are the toilets."

I blinked in surprise. I've had clients seize on unlikely aspects of our country before—everything from our motorcycles to our pop stars—but never had anyone given pride of place to our plumbing.

Her eyes ablaze with sudden interest, Weezie leaned closer. Despite the presence of others in the lobby, she didn't remotely lower her voice as she asked, "So what's with all the different ways to flush?"

I felt the first prickle of embarrassment; still, I had to admit she had a point. When it comes to Italian commodes, you're never quite sure what kind of equipment you'll be using. There's the classic chain attached to the tank; the push-button set in the wall; the pedal; the lever on the flank; the inner cassete with the movable switch; the fully automatic, with no discernible means of command; and, most recently, a new high-tech model that lets you select the appropriate amount of water to handle what you've evacuated.

But I didn't relish dwelling on the subject, so I shrugged it off by saying, "Oh, you know . . . the Mediterranean fantasy."

I wasn't quite sure what I meant by this, but whatever it was, it was insufficient to divert the laserlike curiosity of Weezie Weasle. She gripped my arm and said, "Listen, Marco, can you come with me to the ladies' room for a minute?"

"Um . . . yes," I answered cautiously, "but can I know for what reason?"

"I want to show you something."

Half a dozen lurid possibilities played out in my mind as I

followed her across the lobby to the women's room, then over the threshold into the sanctum sanctorum itself.

Fortunately no one else was within. (Not that the bulldozing Weezie had bothered to check.) I stood just inside the door, not wanting to go any farther, and awaited what came next with a mixture of interest and dread.

Weezie pointed to the far wall and asked, "What's that for?"

I looked where she was pointing. "That's the bidet," I answered.

"Th . . . the bee-*what*?"

I could feel myself reddening. "It's used to wash your . . . your intimate parts."

She looked at me very dubiously, as though I might be trying to pull one over on her. There was an uncomfortable pause while I tried to think of what else I could say to convince her. As you might imagine, nothing leapt immediately to mind. Then she astonished me by saying, "Can you show me how it's done, please? I'd really appreciate it."

I balked and made some excuse, but she was very insistent, and even at the best of times I find it difficult to say no to a beautiful woman. So with as much nonchalance as I could muster, I crossed the room, swung one leg over the bidet, and lowered myself onto it. Then, with my face to the wall, I mimed the whole operation.

The irony of the situation was not lost on me. I had worried that my client's child might not be toilet trained; I'd never considered that there might be a similar issue with the client herself. Nor that I would be the one called on to provide instruction.

I reflected on my preparation for my career as a Chianti tour guide—the weeks of intensive research into local history, tradition, and viticulture. How could I have guessed I should've spared a few hours to brush up on matters of feminine hygiene?

Weezie loomed over me as I went through the appropriate motions, cooing with interest. And just when I was convinced that the situation had reached a pinnacle of mortification, the door swung open and the concierge looked in, with two other men peering over his shoulder. "Ah," he said as I scrambled off the basin, "I thought I saw you come in here."

Weezie was completely unfazed, as though we'd been caught huddling over a brochure instead of a bidet. "Huck, Chet," she said brightly, "this is Franco, our Italian guide!"

"Actually, my name is Dario," I said, extending my hand.

"Oh, right! Dario, this is my husband, Huck"—here I shook the hand of an austere-faced, white-haired gentleman—"and our son, Chet." I looked beyond the husband and saw that the next hand awaiting mine belonged to a man on the cusp of middle age.

It seemed that my van was safe from the incursion of any dirty diapers.

As I led them out of the hotel, I tried to work it out in my head. Weezie's husband was at least seventy, and their "son" no less than forty. I also noticed that Chet was the spitting image of Huck, so their relationship couldn't be doubted. Clearly, then, Weezie was Huck's young trophy wife, taken on late in life (and fairly recently, if her youth was any indication).

Why then did she continue to refer to Chet as "my son"? Why did she persist throughout the day in scolding him as though she were his Italian *mamma*, telling him to put on a sweater, not to drink too much wine, and that he'd had too many sweets? Chet—whom I later learned was a successful trial lawyer—never protested, blithely accepting this bizarre situation. Indeed, whenever Weezie began lecturing him, he produced an old coin and flipped it repeatedly in the air with an expression of serene indifference.

For my part, however, it was very disconcerting to be in their company. I felt like the sole audience member for a play that had been very badly miscast—Britney Spears as Auntie Mame.

Our first stop was the Etruscan ruins. Huck—whom I later learned had been an officer in the marines during Vietnam—was in a sullen, growly mood and responded to nothing I said. Weezie, however, examined the dig so thoroughly that I half expected her to ask where the Etruscans kept their bidet.

Chet, however, seemed fairly agreeable and well balanced, and so on our way back to the van, I deliberately walked beside him. He took advantage of this to apologize for his father, explaining that the old man had slept badly because of a baby crying in the next room. I nodded, and awaited a subsequent explanation for the odd behavior of Weezie. None came.

Chet did, however, remove his trusty coin from his pocket and toss it in the air a few times. Then he handed it to me to look over. "I bought it from a street vendor," he said proudly, "just wandering around the center of Rome. He had a whole case of stuff, if you can believe it—antiquities and whatever. I paid a lot of money, but it isn't every day you stumble across something this ancient."

I gave the coin a cursory look. I'm no expert, so I didn't know what to make of it. "What makes you think it's ancient?" I asked.

"Easy—look below the effigy and you can see the date engraved." He pointed at the face of the coin, lying upright in my palm. "Right there . . . 42 B.C.!" Happily he took the coin back and tossed it in the air again.

We walked several yards in silence while I framed my reply. "Chet," I said quietly, "I have the slight impression that you've been conned."

"What?" he exclaimed. "What makes you say that?"

"Well . . . unless this was minted by a fortune-teller, how could they have known in 42 B.C. that it *was* 42 B.C.?"

He stopped dead in his tracks, a look of horrified enlightenment creeping slowly over his face. Suddenly I began to wonder about the fate of his clients in the courtroom. If he was this slow on the uptake, it wouldn't have surprised me to hear that there were people in California doing hard time for parking tickets.

Weezie had happened to overhear the whole exchange; now she nudged me and said, "Kids today, huh? . . . No street smarts!"

At lunch Weezie fussed embarrassingly over Chet, tucking in his napkin, cutting his meat for him, and generally doing everything short of spoon-feeding him from a jar of stewed beets. It was surreal. Chet bore it all with bemused silence, but he no longer flipped his coin.

Huck, however, had had a few glasses of wine and was now quite recovered from his earlier irritability. He leaned across the table and said, "Dario, we're really enjoying Italy a lot—you know, all the history, and the art, and the culture—and we've visited the most amazing places and seen so much beauty. But there's one thing we just don't get. Right before coming to Tuscany, we visited Pompeii—you know the place I'm talking about? Down south?"

"Yes, of course," I replied; "the city destroyed by Vesuvius in the year 79."

"Exactly!" He seemed excited that I knew what he was talking about. "Well, I can tell you, it was an amazing experience to walk through the ruins of what must've once been a thriving city. And to see the fossilized remains of all those thousands of poor souls caught in the lava . . . Which makes us wonder, how come we didn't hear about this before? You'd think something like this, a tragedy of this size . . ."

His voice trailed away, swamped by sudden emotion; indeed, he seemed so deeply affected that I was taken aback. "Well," I said, "I think it's a *fairly* well-known catastrophe . . ."

He shook his head firmly. "No, Dario. I read the newspaper cover to cover every day—have done for years—and believe me, there was absolutely *no* mention of this disaster in '79."

After this I considered it best to steer the entire party clear of any discussion of Italian phenomena—whether historical or infrastructural—and kept them busy with a stream of questions about their lives back in the States.

On returning to the hotel, Weezie asked if I would get her the train timetables. I agreed, and Chet offered to accompany me to the station. When we reached the ticket office, we stood in line behind two Canadian boys, both strapped beneath enormous backpacks emblazoned with the maple-leaf emblem.

While we awaited our turn, Chet finally consented to talk about Weezie. He confessed that the strange situation with her had by now become absolutely normal to him. At the beginning, of course, it had annoyed him very much; but having seen the deep affection his father had for this woman, he'd decided to grin and bear it. He even agreed to accompany the couple on their annual trips to Europe.

"Honestly," he said with a laugh, "it's not such a big sacrifice, being fussed over by an attractive young girl. I know it must look a bit ridiculous, but no one here knows me anyway."

I still felt I had only half the story. I was trying to find a polite way of asking whether Weezie was playing a game with him, or whether she really was in fact quite mad, when I noticed that the two young Canadians ahead of us were growing increasingly shrill. They were leaning into the window and asking, "Is this a tiai?"

The poor state employee kept shrugging and gesturing to show that he didn't know what they were talking about. Instead of trying a different approach, the youths kept repeating, more insistently, "Is—this—a—tiai . . . IS—THIS—A—TIAAAAI?" At the fifth such attempt, the ticket seller lost his patience and made an eloquent hand gesture to wave them aside. The boys immediately protested. To avert a diplomatic incident, I decided to intervene, even though I myself was a bit irked by the behavior of the boys.

They were very happy to have someone come to their aid. They asked me if this was a "tiai." I told them I didn't know what that meant. They sighed in exasperation and said, "*Tourist Information!*"

It took me a moment to realize they'd been saying, "T.I." Astounded, I exclaimed, "No, it's a T.O." They looked at me blankly. "A ticket office."

I asked them what it was they needed. "Two tickets for Pisa."

"Why didn't you just say so, instead of driving the poor ticket agent crazy with that stupid acronym?"

They shrugged, their eyes growing cloudy with the effort of having to think so hard. I considered how well they'd fit in once they got to Pisa.

Just then a taxi screeched to a halt in front of the station; its back door flew open and Weezie sprang forth. Apparently agitated because we'd been away for more than half an hour, she burst into the station, handbag and hair whipping furiously behind her. When she reached us she grabbed me by the arm and led me away.

Once we were well out of Chet's earshot, she said to me in a low voice, "I'm sorry, Danielo, I shouldn't have gotten you involved in this. I swear I can't trust that boy to do anything. God only knows what a mess he's made of writing down the timetables. It's better if I just take care of it myself."

It was that evening, at home, recalling the events of the day, that I first thought about writing this book.

ALL ABOUT BABS

I have never been to the United States (don't ask for a reason because I don't have one). Thus meeting Americans is my only exposure to the country's social, cultural, and economic realities, so different from the ones I know and live by. Of course, the Americans I deal with don't give me the whole picture, because they're mostly examples of the upper middle class—privileged, moneyed, educated. And since a great number are referrals from previous customers, it ends up that many of my clients come from the same social and professional circles in the same cities. Most of my Chicago clients are Jewish; most of those from Washington are lawyers; those from New York tend to be bankers; those from Los Angeles, journalists. For me Birmingham is a city filled with young people, while Memphis is home mainly to the aged.

Conversely, I play a part in shaping my clients' often distorted image of Italy, usually formed by the movies in the 1950s, which were mainly set in a sensual and backward south. Often when I introduce myself, I see my clients' eyes widen in surprise, no doubt because I am blond and blue eyed. They are, perhaps naturally, expecting a small, dark man with jet-black hair, and maybe even a beautiful mustache in the *picciotto* style, as in *The Godfather*. When they discover that I am not a Catholic, that I do not come from a large family, and that I live with a woman without being married, they are usually a bit dumbstruck. Many still imagine Italy to be a country in which everyone goes to Mass, marriages last forever, abortion is still illegal, and the men go around with a *mandolino* under the arm and a Jew's harp in the pocket.

This tendency to generalize touches everyone, and I admit I'm not immune. To me it's almost become a game: When I encounter new customers, I immediately try to fit them into one of the categories or "types" with which I have become so familiar:

1. *The normal folks*. This, happily, encompasses the majority of my clients. They are always punctual, dress appropriately, ask the right questions at the right moment, eat and drink happily, have a good time, and often remain friends. Strange how during tours with these people the sun always shines, and nothing unpleasant ever happens.

2. *The ghosts*. These, too, are readily adaptable and cause no problems, but differ from the normal folks in that they leave no trace. They are so anonymous that after having taken them back to their hotels I almost immediately forget their faces, and they disappear forever from my life. Usually they are very silent.

3. *The culture vultures*. The members of this category are incredibly ambitious. They ache to know every single story, to see and touch everything. They always have a guidebook in their hands so that they can retain control over where we are and what we're doing. For them the tour becomes a challenge: to see as much as possible in the shortest possible time. To achieve this they assemble

schedules in which they expect to visit Siena, Florence, and San Gimignano in the same day, stopping only for lunch. They force themselves through marathon days, terrible in the end because they go home remembering nothing.

4. *The "babs."* Here you must allow me a few extra lines, because this is the category with which I perhaps amuse myself the most, even if it is the one that leaves me most exhausted. This category is composed of women who travel accompanied by other women—friends, mothers, daughters, grandmothers, granddaughters—but invariably without men. Generally we're talking about well-off women whose husbands or fathers have stayed at home, but sent along several credit cards with no budget limits. In everyday life these women's main occupations are shopping, golfing, playing tennis at the club, shopping, having tea or coffee with friends, browsing through fashion magazines, and shopping. Take away the golf, tennis, and kaffeeklatsch friends, and these women are left with only two possible pursuits in Italy: familiarizing themselves with the latest from the Italian design houses, and then renovating their wardrobe for the upcoming season. They are well versed in every page of every single couture magazine. The cuts, colors, and maquillage of the autumn–winter collections hold for them no secrets; creams and wrinkle-erasing products are their daily bread. And yet, looking at them, you would think they don't know the meaning of the word *style*. They slavishly copy what they've seen on the backs of slender, twenty-something fashion models without taking into account their more advanced age

and size. They sport rigid hairstyles, sticky as cotton candy from excessive hair spray; they pile goop on their eyelashes, bury their faces in layers of powder, and varnish their long nails with garish pink enamels.

To avert unnecessary inconveniences, I'm in the habit of telephoning my customers the evening before a tour to advise them to dress casually. With babs, it's no use. The next morning I invariably have to wait at least half an hour for these women, knowing that when they do appear they'll be dressed and made up as though they were performing on a trapeze. Their favorite outfit—or a least the one they consider most suitable for a country tour—is composed of skintight slacks with jungle cat patterns, glittery blouses, shoes with stiletto heels, very small purses rigorously stuffed, and a great number of giant golden baubles, so large as to seem fake.

Seeing them so often without their husbands, I have formulated two theories:

1. The husband is a hapless victim who, in order to finance his wife's whims, can't afford a vacation himself and has to remain at home and work.

2. The husband is a harried victim who is more than content to finance his wife's vacations so that he can enjoy a period of tranquillity while she is very, very far away.

As soon as the babs meet me, they politely say, "Oh, Dario, we've heard such fantastic things about you!" They pile into my van, drink their first Diet Cokes of the day, and then—after enduring the wear and tear of all this activity—immediately begin replenishing their lipstick with intense rose, red carmine, pomegranate, or any other color recommended by *Vogue* or *Marie Claire*.

Usually these ladies don't like walking and decline even to visit the more accessible sites because they consider it too much effort to get out of the van. At lunch they watch me desolately as I down the appetizers, then the first course, then the second course—they, of course, having nothing more than a few scraps of lettuce on their plates. They also disdain wine, but continue draining Diet Cokes, leaving on the rims of the glasses those terrifying lipstick stains that not even powerful dishwashers can easily remove.

The inevitable question arises: "Dario, how come in Italy everyone eats so much, but you don't see any fat people?" The babs are endlessly fascinated by the idea of staying thin without following absurd and laborious diets. Of course, when confronted with Gina's homemade *tiramisù*, they speedily give in to temptation. After which I know that I must allow a long restroom pause of approximately fifteen minutes per bab—just the time required to reappear completely restored, eyes more deeply set in black, mouths more deeply crimson, as though they've been devouring live animals in the bathroom.

Eventually they will notice that their schedule allows no time for shopping, and with no possibility in sight of spending their money (or more likely their husbands'), their hands begin to itch and twitch.

When I notice the onset of a shopping withdrawal (symptoms include total deafness to my spiel, continual and impatient questions about our route, sudden alertness to anything that might indicate the presence of a store, and a junkie-like need for a can of Diet Coke), I pretend to have a sudden brainstorm: Why don't we stop at a local ceramics shop? . . . The reaction borders on the ravenous; it's like offering a hunk of carrion to starving wolves.

The owner of this shop, Romano Rampini, has built up a successful business selling ceramics to tourists and shipping them all over the world. His inventory includes reproductions of both ancient and Renaissance ceramics, modern objets d'art, and traditional Tuscan pieces. By now there are many who have followed his example, but I prefer to stop at his place because, while I'm not an expert, it seems to me that he sells pieces of very high quality.

From Romano's father, a man with typically dark Etruscan features, I learned that in the past ceramics were used exclusively by wealthy families, while peasants ate their meals on slices of bread (thus explaining the origin of *crostini* and *bruschette*). Every noble family had its own distinct pattern painted on the ceramics, with the color changing according to the importance of the guests who would dine from them. The incredible capper to this story is that, for hygienic reasons, at the end of every meal all those masterpieces were thrown away. Hundreds of artists and artisans had to re-create them continuously.

Because they were luxury items, decorated ceramics are even today considered a bit snobbish and don't inspire much enthusiasm among the locals. My customers, however, take one look at a dazzling shop filled with gorgeously glazed plates, saucers, cups, and vases and immediately come to attention. When Romano pronounces the two magical phrases—"We accept credit cards" and "We ship everything directly to your door"—the babs go almost literally crazy. They begin spinning like tops between the shelves until they've seen and touched everything, and then start firing off demands for all kinds of information and impossible details until the poor store clerks begin to look a bit battered.

Then there's the pathological behavior at the counter. I've

seen some would-be buyers who seemed utterly sold on an array of items turn and leave empty handed, while others who haven't seemed particularly interested in anything suddenly buy entire table sets worth millions of *lire*. Sometimes a bab will take two hours to buy an ashtray, debating over the color on the rim: Will it fit well with her new kitchen, or not?

Often, while driving past the magnificent restored farm-houses, the babs will look at them longingly, dreaming of own-ing one—not because they are particularly fascinated by the building or by the area, but because owning a house in Tuscany is the trend of the moment and therefore such a purchase would give them enormous cachet at the golf club. I shudder to think of the pressure that will be brought to bear on the unsuspecting husbands when these wives get back home.

My days with the babs are often filled with many personal questions, such as "How many times have you been married?" . . . "How many siblings do you have?" . . . "Are your parents still alive?" . . . "What do they do?" . . . "Where do they live?" . . . "If you're not married, are you engaged?" These questions inevitably arise in the most unusual situations—in a church, in a winery, in the middle of the Campo—and almost always occur in the mid-dle of one of my lectures. I am also made to pose for countless photos—close to the van, far from the van, inside the van, close to Gina, embracing Gina, with a wineglass in my hand, without the wineglass in my hand. "Just a bit more to the right, please, Dario" . . . "Move a hair to the left" . . . "Okay, one step backward" . . . "Great! Smile" . . . and so on, for the whole day, even if the shots they seem to prefer are those in which I embrace each one of them in turn.

The typical day with a bab is concluded with a good-bye kiss, which remains imprinted on my face for the whole evening. The day also concludes with my sinking certainty that of the history and culture of Chianti they have learned nothing, but that they've had a good time and will recommend me to other girls at the golf club.

Only once did a bab wish me to extend the tour. She handed me a hundred dollars and asked if I would accompany her to her suite. I was paralyzed for a moment, then handed back the money and politely said, "Sorry, ma'am, but the name of my agency is Rooster Tours, not Cock Tours."

DECEMBER WITH THE COLLEGE STUDENT

The year draws to a close with a month of shortened days in which you must take full advantage of the few hours of daylight.

This is also the time in which the olives are ripe, and everywhere farmers are busy gathering them, picking them from atop ladders, tarpaulins spread on the ground to catch the precious fruits. There is not the same festive spirit of the grape harvest, because this is cold, tedious work. The olives are small and hard, and it seems impossible that they will be able to produce much oil.

Despite the short days, winter still hasn't begun in earnest, and you can still find some determined flowers staking their claim to the surface. Pale roses linger in the garden alongside the omnipresent daisies, and as always the wild marigolds; it's said that if they are still closed by 7:00 A.M., it will rain during the day. Now the woodcutters begin their work, and you can hear in the distance the sound of the chain saws turning trees into logs. Everywhere enormous heaps of firewood accumulate, and after they are seasoned they will be ready to burn brilliantly in the hearth, helping to pass the long winter nights.

On a cold December afternoon, I was strolling through the

crowded streets of Siena, all of which were decked out for the coming holidays. I was feeling good about the way my season had turned out, and looking forward to a few weeks of rest. I happened to pass in front of a rather rough-looking wine bar, and since it was about the right time, and since my stomach was sending me some urgent communiqués, I decided to stop in for a bite to eat and a nice, healthy glass of red wine.

When I entered the small bar, I noticed at once a group of customers seated at a small table, wineglasses ranged around them, waving their hands in the air as they discussed with militant conviction their infallible solutions to the problems facing our planet. They were typical tavern types, those who can be found at the bar all day, every day, engaged in some heated debate, shouting their opinions into each other's characteristically purple-veined, crimson-nosed faces.

I ordered a plate of anchovies in pesto sauce, a couple of slices of ham, and a quarter jug of the better house wine. While the nectar of Bacchus slowly trickled into my stomach, producing the familiar sensations of warmth and spiritual contentment, a young girl entered. By the way she was dressed, I guessed that she was foreign. She wasn't very tall but she was very pretty, with nice chestnut bangs and a beautiful pair of hazelnut eyes.

Very rarely do young, pretty girls enter a bar of this kind. Accordingly, her presence caused an immediate stir among the group of drinkers, who came out with some comments that I prefer not to record. A bit embarrassed, the girl ordered a drink and politely asked in stilted Italian if she could sit with me, since all the other tables were occupied. Of course I said yes, and tried to break the ice with the most banal question I could think of: "What's your name?"

"Carter," she replied, with the kind of pleasant lilt in the voice you usually find in Americans from the southern states. I smiled at the oddity of a young girl bearing the name of a U.S. president. I imagined the incendiary comments my relatives would make if I named a future daughter Scalfaro or Ciampi . . . or, worse, Berlusconi!

After three glasses of wine, the shyness disappeared. Since Carter had found someone with whom she could converse in English, she began relating much of her story to me. She was studying in Siena, but would soon return to the United States for the Christmas break. She was very pleasant company and had a good sense of humor, and would occasionally burst into very loud laughter that made all the people in the small bar turn to look at her. With one glass following another, the time passed quickly; soon we felt slightly tipsy and decided to take a walk through the city center to clear our heads.

The roads were empty. Without realizing it we had stayed in the bar for a very long time, and it was rather a shock when an icy wind raked across our well-warmed cheeks. The air was frigid, but in compensation the sky was crystal clear and full of stars, and the remarkable amount of wine we'd consumed rendered the cold bearable.

We descended the steps that lead to the Campo hand in hand. The square was deserted except for a sole guitarist, who was playing some classic Sienese folk songs. Without saying a word we approached the Mangia Tower, where we were seized by an unrestrainable passion; there, in the moonlight, we kissed repeatedly and tenderly.

We wandered around the city for another hour or so; then Carter turned and gave me one last kiss. When I opened my eyes, she was dashing away. I was stunned and stood rooted to the spot; had I done something wrong? When she was about a hundred yards from me, she stopped and turned just long enough to shout, *"Thanks, Dario, but I've got to go,"* and then resumed galloping away. It was several moments before I realized she'd really bolted, and I was utterly bewildered by this strange behavior. I didn't even know where to go and look for her. All I knew was that she studied in Vermont.

A few days passed, and I received an unexpected telephone call from a hotel in Florence. Even though it was the off-season, a couple of Americans wished to take a tour of the Sienese countryside. The following morning I found myself in the car with a very pleasant middle-aged couple from Alabama. Despite the brusque weather, we spent a splendid day together, until I had the bright idea of asking the reason for their visit to Italy.

"We've come to visit our daughter. She attends the University of Vermont, but she's spending the term in Florence. She was just in Siena for a few days and she spoke so highly of it that we didn't want to miss it." I felt my face start to burn. Could these be Carter's parents? I suddenly felt very awkward and tried to change the subject, but the wife had already had a brainstorm. "You know what we'll do? We'll book you for tomorrow as well, so you can meet her and get to know each other."

"I-I-I don't know," I stuttered. "Perhaps it's not a good idea." But she was insistent. "Oh, come on now, don't be shy! Our Jessica loves meeting new people, and since she's staying here for a while, we'd rest easier knowing she has a friend among the locals."

"Jessica?" I said, repeating the name in relief. "All right, then, ma'am, tomorrow will work out fine."

The next day I picked up the couple and, as promised, they were accompanied by their daughter. Jessica was a graceful girl: long blond hair falling down around her shoulders, emerald-green eyes sparkling from a slightly freckled little face . . . but what struck me most was her sweet, slightly distant voice, which issued like a sigh from her two full lips.

The day passed happily, although I had the uncomfortable impression throughout that Jessica's parents didn't just want me to get to know her but were actually trying to hand her over to me. In the van they made her sit next to me, and when we were out walking they would always follow a few steps behind, as though unwilling to disturb our intimacy. At lunch they sat us next to each other again, and in the evening when we returned, Jessica's mother secretly slipped her daughter's phone number into my pocket and winked. Surely all of this was embarrassing, but given the sweetness and innocent beauty of Jessica, I was more than willing to have a go at making her mother happy.

The following day, despite a very heavy rainstorm, I decided to pay Jessica a visit at her apartment in Florence, armed with a red rose and more than a few hopes. Once I'd dashed from my van up the street to her lodging, I hesitated for a moment before the big wooden door. Now that I'd driven all the way here and gotten soaked to the skin, I wondered how good an idea this was. Hedging my bet, I took out my cell phone and dialed the number her mother had given me. At the third ring Jessica's sweet, dreamy voice responded, and with no small embarrassment I asked if she wanted to go out with me. Unlike many women who respond to this request with feigned uncertainty and a lack of enthusiasm, she immediately cooed a sincere "*Wooooon*derful."

"Even now?" I added.

"*Suuuure,*" she said, still cooing. And so I rang the doorbell. She said, "Wait a second, someone's at the door." When she saw me standing there completely soaked, a rose in one hand and the telephone in the other, she burst into glorious laughter.

For the next two weeks, we saw each other nearly every day. I introduced her to my group of friends, in whose Tuscan accent she became "Jessiha," and in no time her sympathy and sweetness won them all over. Before she returned to the States, we threw a dinner party in her honor, and the day after, with tears in our eyes, I accompanied her to the station. Watching her go was indeed painful. The last image I have of her is a brilliant smile and a good-bye wave from the train window, getting smaller and smaller as the train shot toward the horizon.

Three days later I had my last scheduled tour of the year— three women whom I would pick up in Florence. But when I reached their hotel, I found only two of them waiting for me: the grandmother and mother of a girl who had woken up with a headache and therefore opted out. After we'd left Florence and were on the winding roads of Chianti, the older woman exclaimed, "How beautiful! It reminds me of my beloved hills of Vermont." Hearing that name again, I of course thought about Jessica, and felt compelled to tell the two women that only a few days earlier I had accompanied to the station a girl who, after a stay in Tuscany, was returning to study at the University of Vermont.

"What a coincidence!" the mother said. "My daughter Carter goes to the same school!" She looked back at the grandmother. "Oh, what a pity she couldn't come today."

"She's an adorable girl," said the grandmother, nodding. "You'd have liked her."

I couldn't believe my ears. The coincidence was both stupefying and comical. I could just imagine Carter's sudden "headache" when she heard the name of the guide her mother had hired for the day.

But the surprises weren't over. A month later, Jessica phoned me from Vermont, and I told her the whole story. She started giggling uncontrollably and said, "Dario . . . Carter's my room-mate!"

THE TOUR THAT WASN'T

Over the course of my years as a guide, there have been a few occasions on which, through miscues or mischance, tours haven't worked out as planned. Once I arrived at a remote country house where I was supposed to meet a group of Australian tourists; instead I found a family of Tuscan farmers busy slaughtering an enormous pig. The agency had given me the wrong address. I lost the entire day and my customers, but as compensation I took home enough sausages and salami for a whole year.

On another occasion I had arranged to meet the owners of a travel agency near the exit of a highway at ten in the morning. Three hours later no one had arrived, and I drove home disappointed and confused. Later that afternoon they phoned from the rendezvous point, furious that I wasn't there waiting for them. I protested that I had in fact waited quite a while, only leaving when it became too late in the day to do any kind of tour. "And," I added, "if you're only just arriving, it means I would have had to wait seven hours. Surely you wouldn't expect that of me."

"We got lost," they said, without a hint of apology. "But it was your duty to wait for us! We're sorry, Dario, but you won't be getting any customers for your tours through our agency."

Nor would I want any, I thought with relief as I hung up on the pompous pair.

More recently I met a pair of clients at their villa, as arranged—but the tour was abandoned anyway. The husband, it turned out, had not understood the villa's caretaker, who had warned him the day before—in Italian—that he'd be draining the swimming pool in order to clean it. Accordingly my client got up that morning and, as was his habit, walked out to the pool and dived in. I arrived to find him, bruised and battered, being tended by a local doctor. His wife, too, was badly shaken; there was no question of either of them accompanying me. Only the caretaker seemed unperturbed; he maintained a straight face but was clearly laughing under his breath.

Another thing that used to throw me for a loop was women who reserved a tour under their maiden names, then registered at the hotel under their married names. The first few times this occurred I actually left customers waiting at their hotels simply because at the desk the clerk told me they had no such guests as those I was asking for.

One of my more incredible snafus began the morning I went to Florence to pick up some clients who'd told me they'd be staying at the Astoria Hotel. The concierge, however, told me that there were no guests by that name registered there. I was puzzled and lingered for a while, but could think of no way of salvaging the situation and so went back to my van and started for home. I was well on my way when my cell phone rang; it was my customers. "Dario, what's up? We've been waiting for you in the lobby for over an hour."

"That's impossible," I said. "I was just there. The porter assured me that the hotel had no guests named Randall. You are at the Astoria, correct?" They confirmed that they were. I was sorry for the misunderstanding, but assured them I'd turn right around and fetch them. "However," I warned them, "I may be a while getting back, because at this time of day the traffic in Florence can be a bit heavy."

"Florence?" Mr. Randall said. "But . . . we're in Venice!" From which I have learned, when making appointments and reservations, to take nothing for granted.

"Does your van have air-conditioning, Dario?" Believe it or not, my answer to that question has resulted in the last-minute cancellation of more than one tour. Apparently the lack of forced, chill air is sufficient reason for some to renounce the pleasure of a refreshing Chianti tour. I say *refreshing* because on torrid days, I design the tour to avoid direct sun: I travel only shaded side roads; the Etruscan tombs are immersed in a dense and scented cypress forest; Castle Brolio sits atop a well-ventilated hill; lunch is taken outdoors, under the leaves of a maple tree; and the temperature in the wine cellars never gets above fifty. Even in the van, with the big lateral windows and the two sunroofs open, the drive is breezy and pleasant. Still, some customers are inflexible. Once a middle-aged couple refused to tour with me for this reason, despite the temperature on that autumn day calling more for heating than air-conditioning.

My most notorious nontour happened fairly recently. I was scheduled for a tour with two couples, who had reserved the date a few months before. The Jacobs and the Maxwells were lodged at the Villa de' Santi, a splendid five-star complex in the hills that encircle Florence. When I go to meet customers in these very tony places, I am always a little apprehensive, because often they turn out to be spoiled and difficult, accustomed to having their whims met at a snap of their fingers.

Following my normal routine, I phoned the night before and asked the hotel receptionist if I might speak to one of my customers. "Sure, can you hold on a moment?" he answered, modulating his voice in the manner taught by the best hotel-personnel schools. After a short interval he came back on the line and said that the only person available at the moment was Mrs. Jacob. "The lady is in her room but does not want to speak to you; I'm sorry, but I think you'll have to try back later." Perplexed, I asked if there was any particular reason for this refusal. He said, "No particular reason; she simply doesn't want to talk to you."

I lowered the receiver and experienced a little shiver of dread. These customers were going to be a bad bunch; they were already causing me trouble, and I hadn't even picked them up yet.

After an hour I tried again, and fortunately this time I reached Mrs. Jacob's husband, who enthusiastically said, "Dario, hello! We're friends of the Levis—you took them around Chianti last year, do you remember?"

I answered equally enthusiastically, "Yes, we passed a splendid day together," which was not at all hyperbole. In fact I remembered the Levis fondly: an elderly, energetic, utterly likable couple who gleefully let me guide them around the Tuscan countryside without a moment's difficulty or complaint.

"Great," said Mr. Jacob, "because we'd like to have the same tour you gave them."

"No problem. That means a nine o'clock departure. Be ready in the lobby, and come dressed very casually—sneakers or gym shoes, if you have them." He seemed agreeable, and I hung up feeling much better about the coming tour. Perhaps I'd been too quick to judge them; Mr. Jacob seemed kind and accommodating, and if he and his wife were friends of the Levis, how bad could they be?

After half an hour the phone rang; it was the concierge of Villa de' Santi. "I will now transfer you to Mr. Jacob," he said, "please hold the line."

Mr. Jacob said, "Dario? . . . Listen, my friend, can you please tell me exactly what we're doing tomorrow?"

"Well . . . at your request, we're doing the same tour as the Levis."

"Right. And . . . what is that, exactly?"

I did a double take at the receiver, then said, "I'll pick you up at nine and drive you to Chianti, where we'll visit a modern, high-tech winery and then a small, family-operated one; after which we'll visit an excavation of Etruscan tombs, some medieval villages, and a local castle. Then for lunch you're in for a treat— a feast prepared by my friend, *mamma* Gina. We'll be wandering far from the traffic and the usual tourist routes, and through it all I'll be entertaining you with all sorts of stories and legends about the territory. I'll have you back at the hotel around five."

"Superb," said Mr. Jacob. "Fantastic. We'll have a great time . . . I like you Dario, we're going to become good buddies. See you tomorrow, my friend!"

Toward suppertime the hotel concierge phoned again, and once again transferred me to Mr. Jacob. "Dario, my friend, we'd like to make a small change: Could you shorten the tour slightly and then accompany us to the Gucci store? . . . My wife and Mrs. Maxwell would really appreciate it a lot!"

Well. Apart from the fact that I didn't even know where it was, I had no intention of escorting these women to Gucci. I told Mr. Jacob that if he wished, we could leave a bit earlier in the morning, and I could trim one or two stops from the tour so that we could get back to the hotel after lunch. From there they could get a taxi to take them wherever they'd like to shop.

Mr. Jacob greeted this change with zeal. "It's a deal, my friend! Let's meet at eight thirty."

After supper, while I was relaxing with a hot herbal tea in front of the television, the phone rang yet again. Once more it was still the Villa de' Santi, and obviously once more it was still Mr. Jacob. "Dario, my friend! Sorry about calling so late, but we'd like to make another change. Our wives want to have the whole afternoon free, so we really need to get back to the hotel around eleven."

I was beginning to get a little nervous. I tried to make him understand that even if we left Florence at eight thirty, it would take an hour to reach the Chianti hills, and consequently another hour to return, leaving only half an hour for the tour, which scarcely seemed worth the effort.

Mr. Jacob was undaunted. "Don't worry, my friend, all we need is to see a few vines and we'll be happy."

I was beginning to suspect that it would take quite a bit more than a few vines to make this group happy.

The following morning I woke up around six, to enable me to get to Florence before the rush hour. The sky was overcast and had an expectant feeling about it—as though at any moment it might unleash the kind of gentle yet incessant rain that people found so tiresome, but was so useful for the countryside.

I arrived at the hotel more than an hour early. To pass the time I explored the grounds, which are splendid. The hotel itself had been converted from an ancient monastery perched on a hilltop with one of the most beautiful outlooks on Florence to be found. Encircling the building is an equally fabulous garden, where manicured flower beds and multicolored flowers form geometric patterns, and a surrounding hedge pruned with mathematical precision encloses statues of mythological figures that supply the only hint of disorder.

After I had spent some time strolling through this triumph of color and aroma, a light rain began. I decided the time had come to ask for my clients. I crossed a parking lot filled with limousines and expensive sports cars, where a group of liveried chauffeurs loitered elegantly; suddenly I felt a bit out of place in my old jeans-and-jacket "uniform."

The reception desk is located inside the deconsecrated chapel, which remains virtually as it was centuries ago, with the imposing marble now serving as a table on which to leave brochures and business cards, and the area reserved for the con-gregation serving as a hall. I looked at my watch. It was eight twenty-five . . . close enough. I asked the concierge if he could inform the Jacobs and the Maxwells of my arrival, and that I would be waiting for them at the hotel entrance, in the car. Then I dashed to my van and moved it to the front of the hotel, where my customers could quickly slip inside without getting too wet.

And then I waited.

At eight forty-five they hadn't yet come down.

At nine o'clock . . . no one.

At nine fifteen I thought, *This is getting ridiculous.*

At nine thirty I reentered the hotel and asked the concierge if he had received any word from my customers. "I've just spo-ken with them now. They'll be down in a few minutes." This seemed to me to mean that they might at any moment decamp from an elevator; accordingly, I waited in the lobby for them.

When I found myself waiting alone at ten o'clock, I began to feel a bit irritated. I paced nervously up and down with my hands crossed behind my back wondering whether my best course of action would be simply to leave. At just the time I had convinced myself of this, I heard someone call to me from the stairs: "Dario, my friend, hello—how are you?" It was, of course, Mr. Jacob, approaching me with his hand extended. "The Levis send you many regards. We're so looking forward to this tour! . . . Please excuse the delay, but you know how women are, huh? . . . Takes 'em an age to get ready."

He continued shaking my hand through all this; I took the opportunity to study him up close. He was dressed exactly like a professional golfer; I wouldn't have been surprised to see a caddy shadowing him. He was about fifty-five, balding, and seemed genuinely friendly. "Do you mind if we wolf down a quick breakfast first?" he asked, releasing my hand at last. "You won't object if you know what's good for you; if our wives don't eat something in the morning, they're *unbearable*. We won't be more than ten minutes."

I was so taken aback by this last request that I fell momentarily dumb, and could only with effort manage to nod. He took my hand again, shook it energetically, and said, "We're all so excited about seeing the wonders of Chianti! Haven't talked about anything else for *weeks*." And then he darted away toward the dining hall.

Half an hour later, with no sign of any activity from the dining hall, my patience had reached its end. I went to the concierge, asked for a sheet of paper, and wrote:

Dear Mr. Jacob,

It is now 10:30 A.M., two hours after our appointed
meeting time. As you desired to be back at the hotel by
eleven, I can only conclude that you are no longer interested

in the services I have to offer. I wish you a pleasant day and
much enjoyment during your remaining time in Italy.

Best regards,
Dario (your friend)

I handed the note to the concierge, then turned and headed
for the door. He quickly read it, then ran after me insisting that
I couldn't just go and leave my customers waiting. I pointed out
to him that for two hours, the only one waiting had been me,
and that I would no longer endure this blatant lack of respect. I
was not a chauffeur, hired to be at someone's beck and call, but
a professional with a schedule, and I was going home.

As soon as I left Florence, the rain came harder, to match my
mood. By the time I reached Chianti, it was time for lunch. I
stopped in a local trattoria, where a mammoth steak, a bottle of
red wine, and a local Tuscan cigar restored my good humor.

Later that afternoon, when I arrived home, I noticed that my
voice-mail light was blinking. I played the message:

"Dario, my friend! . . . We're ready. It's eleven thirty . . .
Where are you?"

CONCLUSION

La Macia

I'd gotten up early because the owner of the olive press didn't tolerate his clients arriving late for the pressing. I had no intention of rubbing him the wrong way, especially since it was my olives he would be turning into precious extra-virgin olive oil. I jumped into the van, already filled with the valuable load, and drove directly to the olive mill.

I took a shortcut, full of bends and curves, that runs through the woods and vineyards, crosses over a small bridge, skirts an old flour mill, then ends up back on the main road. As soon as I'd crossed the bridge, however, I noticed something I hadn't seen before, despite having driven this route countless times: a farmhouse, sitting just above me, slightly hidden by the trees. I slowed down to take a longer look at it, and realized that it was visible only because of the naked autumn trees, through whose barren branches I could glimpse the run-down facade and wide-open windows. It was obviously uninhabited.

Suddenly I was thrown back twenty years, seized by the same rush of excitement that possessed me when I was a teenager on my scooter, stumbling across some old farmhouse, long abandoned and unexplored.

Sticking my neck out the window, I saw that to reach this new house all I had to do was to cross a small stream and climb up through the small thicket of oak. I longed to do just that, but I reined myself in: first I had my olive oil appointment.

I parked on the square in front of the press, opened the back of my van, and handed over my precious crop to the owner, who greeted me with a friendly grunt, satisfied by my punctuality. At this point all I had to do was to wait until the old granite millstones had done their job.

I wasn't alone. With me were some of the most renowned characters of the area, all waiting to go home with their oil. Leaning with his back against the stone wall was Zambone, the most feared hunter of the area, reportedly so strong that he can carry two wild boars under his arms (the legend doesn't specify whether the beasts are alive or dead). He was fondling his goatee nervously while chatting with Tanacca, a mate of his from both the hunt and the tavern. I couldn't hear their words over the hubbub of the machinery, but I knew that the possible subjects were limited to the quality of the oil, the last boar hunt, football, and women. Tanacca, a fierce *mangiapreti* (literally "priest eater"—an anticleric), was filling his lungs with cigarette smoke and undoubtedly letting out a stream of obscene expletives, of which he possesses a remarkable repertoire.

In the meantime Mario entered—and judging by the way he was dressed, he had been scouting for mushrooms. He looked around and, seeing me, politely nodded hello. Tall and wiry, always bent forward, Mario is very shy and short on words. He lives alone with his aged mother. Some months before, I had met him at a bar, and while we were having a grappa together, he told me of his passion for making art. I grew curious as he grew increasingly animated, so much so that despite his initial reluctance I persuaded him to show me his work.

I was incredulous: His house was filled with graceful sculptures carved from old tree trunks and oil paintings worthy of an academy graduate. But Mario has never studied; he is a natural talent, a minor Michelangelo hidden away between the walls of his humble home.

Gazza's oil was ready, and he was loading his three shanks into his Fiat Fiorino when Zambone and Tanacca, for no particular reason, started teasing him. Gazza is everyone's target. He lives on his own and is considered a bit of the village fool. Every evening he falls asleep in one of the uncomfortable chairs at the bar, with the TV still blaring at him. Suddenly he'll just go limp, his head lolling back and his mouth hanging open; and then, without fail, the younger patrons will amuse themselves by dropping bits of paper down his throat, until one ends up in his windpipe and, suffocating, he'll wake up in a panic, knocking over his chair and sometimes the table, to the general hilarity of the small crowd of spectators who never miss this show.

These spectators are the same boon companions who one day made Gazza believe that if he ventured into the woods under a full moon ringing a cowbell, porcupines would dash obediently into his open sack. Gazza went out that night to give it a try; his "friends" lay in wait for him behind some trees, then ambushed him with buckets of water, soaking him from head to toe. Poor Gazza never knew what hit him. The following day at the bar, they asked him how the porcupine hunt had gone.

"The moon was full," he said, "and I rang the cowbell and the sack immediately filled up with porcupines. So I started back when suddenly it started raining very hard." The others started laughing, and Gazza protested, "No, really hard! Bucketsful!"

"So what did you do?" his friends asked.

"Well, what do you think? I ran home!"

"But Gazza, where did you put the catch?" asked Zambone mischievously. "Why don't you show it to us?"

"I can't," Gazza said with a sigh. "All the porcupines ran off . . . I realized later the sack had a hole in it."

Gazza now finished loading his oil, hopped behind the wheel, and escaped further taunting from Tanacca and Zambone. His van cut in front of Tonio, who was just now arriving on his trusty bicycle. Tonio hadn't brought any olives; he'd just dropped by to see who was around and exchange a few words. "Hey there, Tonio," I greeted him, "how's life?"

"Very well, Dario," he said proudly. "Very well indeed. Last night I even satisfied my wife!"

Nothing remarkable about this exchange . . . except that the boastful husband was then ninety-four years old.

He's also tiny enough to pass for a forest elf. He retains a thick head of bright white hair, though he usually tucks it under a blue beret. He doesn't have the tired, rheumy eyes of most of his contemporaries, nor their timeworn stoop; he stands erect, shoulders back. True, his cheeks are mapped by a network of scarlet capillary veins, dense as roots, but he still has all his teeth despite (as he'll proudly tell you) the fact that he has never once been to a dentist or allowed a toothbrush into his mouth.

"My wife," he said with a glint in his eye, "you should have seen how she—"

"Yes, yes, okay," I said, interrupting him, knowing full well that he would have entered into a very intimate recounting of his amatory performance. To change the subject I said the first thing that came to mind: "Tonio, don't you think we're getting a bit tight in this press? There are so many of us in here that maybe they should think of enlarging it."

"Eh, *nini*," he replied, using the term of endearment the elderly use to address those younger. "We could do like they did in Monteciocchi, eh?" We sat outside together, where he took from his worn flannel jacket a tin of local cigars. He lit one, puffed it to get it going, and launched into a narration.

"You must know, *nini*, that in the small village of Monteciocchi before the great war lived about forty people, not like today when only how many remain—five? No more than five—but because the church had been built when there were about twenty souls, it happened one day that the townspeople realized they were getting a bit tight in there. The pews no longer had room for everyone, and one of the women who was pregnant pointed out that soon the number of the worshipers would increase even more. The *monteciocchini* decided to meet to discuss the problem, and after the Mass they gathered. The parish priest, knowing that the coffers were nearly empty, immediately dismissed any idea of building a larger church.

"'So what can we do?' they all wailed in disappointment.

"'Easy,' said the lumberjack, who was famous for having a solution to every problem. 'Let's pool our resources.'

"'But,' the miller protested, employing an old Tuscan saying, 'what if altogether we don't have one to make two?'

"The lumberjack said, 'I don't mean financial resources—I mean our physical ones. If each of us leans against the wall and we start pushing with all our might, eventually the walls will widen.'

"Everybody thought this a fine idea, and so the following Sunday, as soon as the Mass ended, they all got busy. They lined up around the interior of the church and pushed mightily. After about half an hour, they went outside to check the result, but they couldn't see any change.

"'Maybe,' said the cobbler, 'the wall *has* moved a few inches, but how can we know for sure?'

"'I have an idea,' said the ironmonger's wife. 'Let's take off our jackets and lay them around the church at the exact point we want the walls to reach.' The idea seemed sound, and so after having doffed their jackets they went back into the church and started pushing with even more enthusiasm.

"In the meantime a thief happened to pass and, seeing all those unguarded jackets neatly lined up on the ground, thought it was his lucky day. He picked them up, one by one, piled them in his arms, and took them all away.

"Around midday the faithful, tired and hungry, came out for a bite to eat before resuming their labors; but as soon as they were outside, they were astonished to find that their jackets were nowhere to be seen.

"'We did it!' exclaimed the lumberjack. 'We pushed the walls so far that we buried our jackets!' And so the *monteciocchini* were satisfied; in the end the price for a larger church had been just a few garments. Happy and content, they organized a great feast and invited the inhabitants of all the neighboring villages."

As Tonio related this tale, a small crowd had gathered to listen, because he was famous in the area for his stories. His audience laughed and applauded appreciatively, and Tonio smiled as he lit another cigar.

Just then I heard someone call my name. My oil was ready. I said good-bye to Tonio, shook his skeletal hand, and thanked him for the company.

One of the things that I enjoy most in life, and that gives me the greatest satisfaction, is new oil. It comes out of the press with a thick, pungent aroma, firmly fruited with a trace of spice, intensely dark green in color and somewhat cloudy, and distinctly flavored, with a tinge of pepper that tickles the throat.

Gradually the oil will become clearer, the taste will become smoother, and it will lose the first bloom of its freshness, becoming similar to the oils found in the supermarket.

I thanked the owner of the press, thinking that I didn't envy him whatsoever the herculean amount of work he had to take on at this time of year. His black-ringed eyes were eloquent testimony to its effects.

I loaded my six stainless-steel, fifty-liter containers into the van and hit the road, licking my lips at the idea of the *bruschette* I would wolf down before the fireplace that night, together with Cristina and a bottle of red wine.

I decided to retake the shortcut along the river and stopped where I had spotted the old farmhouse. I parked the van on a small clearing at the side of the road. The stream was about ready to overflow due to the heavy autumn rainfall, but with a running start I could easily clear it. I backed up, set off at a good clip, then launched myself into the air, and . . . *splash!* Just a few inches and I would've made it; alas, I found myself now ankle deep in muddy water.

With my shoes now soaked and oozing, I climbed up the ravine, then managed to make my way through a dense blackberry bush without ripping my jeans.

Cold, wet, and covered with scratches, I at last reached the farmhouse. The stable and some less important outbuildings had collapsed, the ancient beams unable to survive the years of negligence, but the house itself was upright and sturdy. Above the entrance was a fascist inscription dating from World War II, and despite the many years that had passed, I could read it clearly: VIVA IL DUCE VIVA IL RE IMPERATORE (LONG LIVE THE COMMANDER, LONG LIVE THE KING EMPEROR). The building was, of course, all stone, but parts of the facade were plastered to fill in what seemed to be bullet holes; evidently the house had been the scene of some kind of conflict. Perhaps it had been a partisan hideout . . . ?

All I had to do was find a way in. The front steps were submerged in tangled brambles, but in back I found a second entrance. With a bit of fear, I mounted the rickety stairs, and when I reached the landing, I put some slight pressure on the door; it opened without the slightest creak. As I stepped across the threshold, my attention immediately fell on a beautiful, gigantic fireplace crossed by a massive chestnut beam that, judging by its array of gaping holes, had hosted numerous generations of woodworms.

To my great surprise I saw that some embers were still glowing; on the floor there was a scattering of cigarette butts and a wine flask, recently opened. I heard a dim noise coming from the next room. I froze.

The door swung open and a teenage couple peered in at me apprehensively; apparently I had startled them as much as they had me. With his head low and a slight stutter, the boy said, "Sorry, we d-didn't have any intention of—"

"It's okay," I reassured them, "you aren't trespassing. This house is pretty obviously abandoned, isn't it?" I extended my hand and continued, "My name is Dario. I noticed you've got a fire going; if you don't mind, I'll take advantage of it to dry my feet." I sat on one of the benches inside the fireplace, and the two youngsters, Massimo and Rebecca, sat across from me. Only the fire divided us.

Because of me, they'd passed an anxious fifteen minutes, but now that they had relaxed, we got to know each other. They were seventeen, both attending their last year at the Art Institute in Siena. They'd been using the house as their private hideout for two years! I listened to them with tenderness, catching a glimpse of myself two decades before, not only in what they were telling me but even in the look of their clothes, curiously close to how I had dressed at their age, despite the arrival of many trends and fashions in the intervening years.

What marked them as modern teenagers were their tattoos and piercings, in my day totally unheard of in Italy. At the beginning of the 1980s, my single earring had branded me as ambiguous and suspect; they, with their multiple earrings and pierced noses, lips, and tongues, probably passed unobserved.

Rebecca was very gracious and had a raucous voice that I thought very sexy. Her wavy black hair had almost blue highlights and fell on tiny shoulders; she was very skinny but well proportioned. She had a slight squint that made her light blue eyes glint with gold, and a prominent nose that gave her the aspect of a serious girl with a good head on her shoulders.

Massimo, on the other hand, looked more like a scamp, his rascally eyes filled with deviltry. He was trying without much success to cultivate a kind of beard at the end of his long, sharp face. He wore his hair straight, uncombed, and dyed a very unnatural shade of orange. Tall and wiry, his hands were long and slender, with the agile fingers of a piano player.

While he passed me a rather too full glass of wine, sloshing a few drops over the crackling flames, I noticed that both of them had paint stains on their clothes and hands. Massimo and I raised our glasses in a toast; Rebecca did not drink.

I talked a bit about myself, about my old passion for

abandoned farmhouses, and about my work. They remained particularly fascinated by my stories of Chianti in the 1970s, of the feasts in the old houses, about the transformations the territory had recently undergone. They told me that their friends differed vastly from mine; they didn't know anyone who spent their spare time in the countryside or even outdoors, everyone preferring to navigate the Internet rather than old stone roads. "But we love all of this," said Massimo, "and would like to do something to maintain it the way it is." They told me that they had eagerly participated in some anti-globalization marches, but since riots and violence had become the norm for such occasions, they'd given it up. "How can it be possible," Massimo said, "that people go to these peace marches armed with iron bars? And then expect it not to end in street warfare?"

"Anyway," added Rebecca, who seemed at last to overcome the initial shyness my presence had provoked in her, "we don't come here just to have our own corner of the world. We have a project we're working on here." I was intrigued, but before I could ask them about it, Massimo stood up and said, "It's getting a bit late, the sun's about to set, and our motorbike is on the other side of the woods."

I decided to go as well. The flames were now dying, so it was safe to leave the fireplace as it was. But the embers had warmed us so thoroughly that when we stepped outside, the frigid air passed through us like a knife.

"So," said Massimo eagerly, "see you tomorrow?"

I shrugged. "Sure. See you tomorrow."

Our paths divided; they cut toward the inside while I descended the ravine through the path Massimo pointed out to me and then, to avoid getting wet again, crossed the current by jumping zigzag over some stones covered in moss. The frogs were croaking, and I heard in the distance the young couple's two-stroke engine start. Then the sound swallowed up by the Chianti woodlands.

On the way back it occurred to me that up to tonight, Massimo and Rebecca's generation had been a blank to me. I was surprised to realize how little contact I'd had with anyone younger than me.

Massimo had impressed me as being a true *chiantigiano*. Not only was his speech of this area, but his body language and hand gestures were typical of the hills. Rebecca, however, spoke with a strange accent that sometimes sounded Tuscan, especially given the number of idiomatic expressions she used; every now and then, though, she'd emit telltale intonations, as when she pronounced certain vowels slightly too openly.

After I crossed the old bridge, where the bend curves tightly toward the left, my thoughts were interrupted by the sudden appearance of a shadowy figure proceeding slowly on a bicycle. My headlamps soon revealed it to be good old Tonio, finally going home. I stopped to give him a lift.

"Eh, *nini*," he said as I loaded his bike in the back of the van, "I guess I talked too much at the press. It's about time I put a light on this bike."

"Listen, Tonio," I asked as we slipped into the front seat, "what can you tell me about that old house—the one on the other side of the stream, with the fascist writing on it?"

The old man didn't answer at first. He fetched his tin box from his jacket, removed a *toscano* cigar, wet it, and lit it with a wooden match. Only after the first puff did he say, "Bad story, my dear Dario . . ." And then he fell silent.

After a few more miles, he said, "Let's stop at the bar; it'll be easier to talk with a glass of red wine in my hand."

He again remained silent until we entered the bar and were seated at a green plastic table in a disgusting 1980s style. Then I noticed the sad veil that had descended over his face. "Very terrible story, that one," he muttered.

I waited for him to continue. After our wine arrived he said, "In that house lived some honest people . . . a beautiful family, hard workers . . ."

He gave the impression of having difficulty getting started, which was odd, because telling stories was his daily bread. Then, after tossing back the entire contents of his glass in one swig, he seemed emboldened, and began again.

"The house you saw was once inhabited by a family of sharecroppers, of whom there were many in those years. They worked the land and looked after the animals for the landowner without worrying what happened in Rome or the rest of the world. Then the war broke out, and the son was sent to die in one of those ice-cold countries during Italy's disastrous campaigns in Russia, and the father joined the partisans. Life is strange, eh, *nini*?" He sighed and continued. "The son fighting for Mussolini, the father against, but how can we judge . . . those were ignorant people. What did they know about words like *fascism* or *communism*? They had only ever known about plowing the fields.

"The mother remained at home with two daughters and her elderly father and mother-in-law. Hard times even for her; there was a lot of misery. The husband became an outlaw, wanted by the fascists. Toward the end of the war, he took part in an action against the retreating Nazis: They blew up a bridge, forcing the Germans to leave the greater part of their weaponry on this side of the bank.

"Then the poor woman hid an English soldier in her house.

He'd been sent ahead as a spy and was injured. He must have reminded her of her son, alone in the Russian winter, and so she took him in.

"When the Germans found out, they went to the farmhouse and . . ." He stopped.

"What did they do?" I asked, completely absorbed by the story.

Tonio stared deeply into my eyes and said with a firm voice, "They killed the whole family, without any pity. They dragged them out, lined them up against the wall right below the fascist graffiti, and machine-gunned them down. Nobody knows for sure what happened to the English soldier, but I heard it whispered that the day before he'd fled and reunited with his companions." He remained completely still for a few moments, seemingly staring through me, then added, "The war was about to end, so those cowards got their revenge on a helpless mother, her two daughters, and two old people. I told you it was a terrible story."

"What happened to the father?" I asked.

"Well . . . the father took many years to recover from the tragedy, but he managed to build a new life for himself. He remarried and even had another son. But surely he carries that terrible wound in his heart to this day."

When I got home I lit the fire. As soon as there were enough embers, I put the grill in place and toasted some homemade bread. I passed the rest of the evening with Cristina, tasting the new oil; it was superb. In fact it was so good that we ended up dining on nothing more than bread, oil, wine, and a few slices of cheese, all the while watching the wood burn away and discussing my strange day. We went to bed very late.

The following morning I decided to return to the abandoned farmhouse.

Before getting into the van, I found a note on the windshield. The handwriting was that of an elderly person.

> I know that today you will return to La Macia (for that is the house's name). On the old brick well, you will find a black stone, different from the others. Move it and you will find something.
>
> Tonio

I jumped in the van and, ignoring all speed limits, raced to the ravine. I parked, crossed the stream, and climbed up through the oak thicket until, panting heavily, I reached La Macia.

In the air there was a strong scent of rotting leaves. I turned toward the barn, then back again—there was the well. I approached, my heartbeat stopping up my ears. I had already spotted the darker stone.

I knelt down, grabbed hold of its two protruding parts, and pulled. Despite all the years, it slipped away instantly. In the cavity behind it, there was a rusty tin tobacco box. I pulled hard on the lid and with only a little effort flipped it open. Within it was a small object wrapped it cloth. I unfolded the cloth to reveal a small wooden frame containing a photograph of a group of people gathered in front of the farmhouse, with the date inscribed: 1937. It was almost certainly the family who had lived here during the war, whom Tonio had told me about.

Above the heads of these people were written their names, as was customary in those days. The grandfather was Adamo; the grandmother Clelia; the daughters Giovanna and Adele; the son Vittorio; the mother Claretta.

"Oh my God," I muttered as I read the husband's name: Antonio. How stupid I had been not to see it before—in Tonio's reluctance to speak of this family, in his obvious emotion.

I was overwhelmed by a wave of guilt. I felt that I had awakened in that old man memories that he had perhaps spent years trying to bury. I replaced the photo in the box and tucked it into my pocket.

Now that the house had a name and a story, even its aspect seemed to be different from the day before, so much so that I felt uneasy approaching it—as though I were somehow unworthy. I examined the holes in the wall, aware that the terrible event Tonio had related to me probably occurred on this very spot. Yet I was unable to picture so violent a scene in so peaceful a setting.

The roar of a motorbike brought me back to reality. It was Massimo and Rebecca, of course. We greeted each other, then lit the fire and sat down in the same spots as the day before. They had brought bread and ham and were happy to share it with me.

After this light lunch and a glass of wine, they told me that they were painting a mural on the walls of the next room, and that they would be happy if I would be the first to see it. They led me through the door. I was overwhelmed by the explosion of color that covered three walls and the ceiling. It was dazzling. "This is the fruit of two years of work," Rebecca said proudly. "We hope it survives here intact, like a message in a bottle . . . a message of peace and love."

"You see," Massimo continued, pointing out certain figures in the mural, "it's our story. Rebecca comes from Albania. Three years ago her parents decided to save her from that country's hunger and misery by putting her on a secret refugee boat. After a disorienting journey it washed up on a beach down south, in Puglia. Rebecca and the others were rounded up by the Italian authorities and put in a special camp till they could be returned to Albania. But somebody did a news story on the refugees that aired on TV, and Rebecca was shown in close-up. That's where I first saw her, and the bereft look on her face tormented me all night long—so much so that the next day I gathered up my few savings and caught the first train to Puglia. When I arrived I tried to get to the refugee camp, but it was impossible: It was guarded by the military as though it were some sort of prison.

"Luckily I found a doctor who was on his way in, and I begged him to let the girl who'd arrived two days before come out to the exit gate. Maybe my youth inspired some compassion in him, I don't know, but he did even better: He took me in with him, pretending I was his son.

"I found Rebecca sitting beneath an olive tree. She was even more beautiful than she was on TV. The rest of the story you can imagine: the phone call to my parents for their help—naturally they were worried and a little incredulous; my persistence against the inevitable roadblocks; Rebecca's removal from the camp and temporary reassignment to a friend's home; and then the great help: My *papà* brought her whole family over and gave Rebecca's father a job in his ceramics factory." Every detail of the story had been reproduced on the wall. It had clearly required meticulous, patient work, but the final result was surprising and moving.

They were gratified by my awed expression. "We've left the last wall empty to paint something different," Rebecca asked. "Do you have any ideas?"

In an instant I knew my answer. "Yes, I do."

We went back to the hearth and sat, and I told them Tonio's story. At the conclusion, when I took the photo from my pocket and showed it to them, Massimo leapt to his feet. "Fantastic!" he cried with all the instantaneous passion of a seventeen-year-old. "We could reproduce that photo with our airbrush over the whole surface of the wall, and then bring your friend up to see it!"

"Mm," I said dubiously, "I don't know if he'd be willing to come back here." Their faces fell, and I felt like a cad for dampening their enthusiasm. I quickly added, "But we can always try. You start working, and I'll see what Tonio has to say about it."

That evening I found Tonio watching a couple of old men playing a hand of *briscola* beneath the bar's neon lights. When he saw me he smiled.

"Don't say anything," I said, anticipating him. "I just want to know two things from you: first, whether you want to see the photo again. And second, if you'd like to go back to La Macia. Maybe we could go together."

He shook his head. "No, *nini*," he said, smiling, "the photo you can keep. I've had my own image etched in my mind for more than sixty years. Surely the one in your pocket is fading while mine remains perfect." Then with a hint of melancholy he added, "But I think I would like to return before I die. I promised myself I would go, but haven't yet found the courage. Maybe now is the time . . . if you would be so kind as to accompany me. Next Thursday would have been my wife's birthday. Maybe that would be a good day."

I was excited by his unexpected acceptance. "Sure, Tonio. I'll come and pick you up. Don't worry."

The kids worked diligently every day to get the painting completed in time, and despite the rush they did a fine job: The image from the old photo now occupied the entire surface of the room's fourth wall.

We reached La Macia before sunset. Tonio by now had gained confidence and decided to enter first. When he saw the fire lit and the table laid, he was visibly moved. "Just like all those years ago . . . when I would return from the fields."

I introduced him to Massimo and Rebecca, and they excitedly accompanied him to see the gift they had prepared. Tonio stood, speechless and still, contemplating the portrait of his family for several very long minutes. Then he looked at us with a kind of ecstatic satisfaction, and said, "At last we have all come home."

That evening was memorable. We spent it dining by candlelight and roasting chestnuts on the fire, just like in the old days. Then Rebecca said that the time had come for her to have her first glass of wine, so we moved to the fireplace and drank to our health: all of us so very different and yet so closely entwined; three generations of *chiantigiani*, raising their glasses before the fire.

EPILOGUE

From the Other Side of the Van

by Robert Rodi

There's a lot that is familiar to me in the preceding chapters. You see, I'm one of Dario's American clients. True, over the years we've become friends—he's almost like a brother to me now—but in the beginning, when my partner Jeffrey and I hired him for the first time, we knew little about Italy, and nothing about him. What, I have often wondered since, did he make of us, as we—in typically American fashion—supplied him with our entire life stories on the twenty-yard walk to his van? I know what we made of him: confident, handsome, easygoing, intelligent, and—above all—reserved. Americans of my class (middle) and age (baby boom) have a peculiar pathology: confession. We spill it all in one big gush. Then, lest anything be lost, we spill it all again. (If possible, we spill it on television.) These waves of too-much information broke against Dario as against a stone promontory. He seemed utterly unaffected. Certainly they inspired in him no urge to reciprocate. By the end of our first day with him, we knew quite a lot about Chianti and virtually nothing about him.

Dario's reserve, as it happens, is of the most attractive kind to vulgar Americans like us: It's Old World. He's a gentleman in the original sense of the word. Over the next few days, this bulwark of reserve began slowly to erode as we proved ourselves worthy of his confidence by embracing enthusiastically the food, the wines, and the entire culture to which he introduced us—in particular, I think, by our immediate and enduring reaction to the city of Siena. We just plain fell for it. Once through the Porta Romana, trekking across that vast carpet of roseate stone to the Campo, we knew we had found a place to which we would return again and again, with ever-greater affection. Siena, like Florence, is an extraordinarily masculine city. Where arrogant Florence wears its beauty like armor, though, Siena's is like the muscles on an athlete. It has both sinew and grace.

As Dario's reserve was waning, it also suffered a few unexpected blows. He took us to see the monks at Sant'Antimo, arriving roughly four minutes before the chanting concluded. He was very embarrassed and apologized profusely. (We've since gone back and attended the full service. Twice, in fact.) He drove us to Castle Brolio, lecturing us en route about the things we would see there. Castle Brolio was closed when we arrived. More abashed apologies. (We've since been back—three times. And yes, the vista is all Dario says it is.)

The greatest compliment I can pay him is that, by the time these snafus occurred, they scarcely mattered. By his serene unflappability, his casual expectation that even our lunches would be three-hour affairs, his complete integration into the imperturbable rhythms of an ancient countryside—by these means he had long since had taught us that the way to know

Chianti is not to race about its sights and scenes, engraving them on your memory (or, more likely, videotaping them to look at later). The way to know Chianti is to take what it gives you with gratitude and pleasure. Castle Brolio is closed? . . . Let's have a drink somewhere and let the sun beat on our faces.

We went home changed men. By the time we returned, we had begun studying Italian and had learned enough to laugh at the newspaper headlines poking fun at *pisani*. We also returned to the States bearing forty-three bottles of wine (and five of olive oil). I almost dislocated my shoulder carrying on a cabin bag filled with illicit Brunello. At this point Dario must have known he had made some serious converts.

His reserve was well and truly gone by July 1997 when we returned, with several friends, for our first Palio. He had obtained a series of windows overlooking the Campo, and we were very well situated for the race. Dario himself, however, was in a state of some agitation. He was very involved with the Caterpillar *contrada*, and the Caterpillar was racing that day. He wore the *contrada* scarf constantly, and in solidarity we all donned it as well. We even tried—difficult, for Americans—not to wear ours ironically.

Dario's usual routine was to meet us at our hotel and then conduct us to whatever location or activity he'd chosen for the day. But on the day of the Palio, he wasn't up to it. We awaited him in the hotel lobby for some time, contenting ourselves with steaming cups of espresso and trying to decipher the day's headlines. Eventually we were called to the telephone. Dario was unable to collect us. Would we be so kind as to take our own car to the restaurant he had chosen for lunch? He provided explicit directions and said he would meet us there. We were more than happy to accommodate him because, thrillingly, we sensed we had come up against a chink in the Dario Castagno armor.

We drove to the countryside and located the charming *ris-torante* where, Dario had assured us, he would be waiting for us. He was not there waiting for us.

But he had phoned ahead and alerted the staff to our arrival. They showed us to a table and began to serve us. We protested that the final member of our party hadn't arrived, and they said, "Not to worry, Dario asks that you begin without him. He will be here shortly."

The five of us dived into our antipasti and *vino da tavola*, but our minds weren't on the repast. We were obsessed and excited by Dario's continued failure to appear. Jeffrey and I were the only drinkers in the group, so we had no doubt as to the cause of his dereliction of duty, while the others took rather silly flights of fancy more indicative of their own fantasies about him than anything else. When he did arrive some time later, his skin was approximately the color of ash, and his eyes were crosshatched with red. He was the very picture of morning-after agony. We sat up brightly at his arrival, because to please him we had all donned our Caterpillar scarves. He seemed not to notice this. I realize now this was because he could not see.

He sat down, propped his head in his hands, and mumbled some apologies before lurching into a halting recital of his debaucheries the night before at Caterpillar headquarters. The phrase I remember best is "shots of flaming grappa." Apparently there had been a lot of them. I can't be sure of the number, because neither was Dario.

One member of our party was a woman of great (in my opinion excessive) volubility, who had known Dario longer than Jeffrey and I and at times acted as though he were her personal property. She had a habit of beginning every sentence with his name. I noticed now that every time she did this, he flinched as though stung. As one familiar with lethal hangovers, I said to this nondrinker, sotto voce, "Look, hon, he's obviously in acute pain. We should lay off him for a while, okay?" She looked back at me, smiling, nodding, in every way oozing agreement. Then thirty seconds later: "Dario . . ."

Later that day, after he had somewhat recovered, we took our position at the windows overlooking the Campo.

Dario talked us through the gorgeous medieval procession that precedes the race. Then, as the jockeys rode out of the Mangia Tower to a deafening roar of acclaim, he said to us, "After the race I will take you to the winning *contrada's* church so you can see the celebration. Unless the Caterpillar wins, and then I must leave you at once." I like to think he wouldn't have felt comfortable telling another group of clients he intended to abandon them in this way. But we knew how important this was to him. And besides, by that time we were feeling really *very* Sienese.

The race was perhaps the single most exciting two minutes of my life. For a few moments God hiccuped, and the law of gravity stopped working. The speed, violence, din, and sheer splendor were very nearly overwhelming—but even more so was the elated sense of community. The spirit of the *polis* lived again in the Campo, and it was the *polis* at play. Dario is right: The Palio *is* Siena.

The Caterpillar didn't win. The Giraffe did. The Giraffe, Dario explained, had once been the Caterpillar's bitter rival, but now there was a treaty between them. From the baleful look on his face, I didn't get the impression the treaty was worth much.

On our fourth visit we engaged Dario again. But by this time he had already shown us, several times, the high points of his

Chianti tour. He suggested something different: a walking tour of the countryside. His dog tagged along—it was that informal. In the course of the walk, we came across, and explored, a number of the abandoned farmhouses Dario discusses with such loving respect in these pages. Until I read those chapters, I didn't know how much such old structures meant to him, and am now all the more honored that he shared them with us. The last time we returned—again with friends, in September 2000 for the Palio Straordinario (a special third race, in honor of the Holy Year)—so much was wonderfully familiar: the rolling, verdant hills of Chianti; the snow-white nave of Sant'Antimo; the unpretentious elegance of Montalcino; the eardrum-rattling roar of the *contrada* anthems being belted out by a thousand voices in unison. And equally familiar was Dario himself. He and Cristina invited our entire party to dinner at their house. Glasses were raised; laughter rang out; corks littered the tabletop; and outside, a drenching rain swept in, then swept out again, attracting only the scarcest notice.

A day later, Dario told me of his plans for this book and asked whether I would lend him a hand with it.

I said yes . . . without reserve.

ABOUT THE AUTHOR

Dario Castagno was born in England to Italian parents and moved with his family to Tuscany when he was ten. Through his company, Chianti Rooster Tours, he has guided small groups of visitors—mostly Americans—to his favorite spots in the Chianti region for more than ten years. This is his first book. Perhaps his proudest accomplishment, however, is claiming membership in Siena's  Caterpillar *contrada,* which in 2003 won the *Palio,* the wildly popular bareback horse race that consumes the energies of the Sienese people each summer. For pictures of the 2003 Palio and more, visit Dario's Web site at www.toomuchtuscansun.com.